scandinavian
QUILT STYLE

scandinavian
QUILT STYLE

Over 40 sewing projects for home comfort and style

Trine Bakke

David and Charles

www.rucraft.co.uk

A DAVID & CHARLES BOOK

© J. W. Cappelens Forlag AS
Cappelen Hobby
www.cappelen.no
Originally published in Norway
as *Lappesaker*

First published in the UK and USA in 2011
by F&W Media International, LTD

David & Charles is an imprint of F&W
Media International, LTD
Brunel House, Forde Close, Newton
Abbot, TQ12 4PU, UK

F&W Media International, LTD is a
subsidiary of F+W Media Inc.
4700 East Galbraith Road, Cincinnati,
OH 45236, USA

A catalogue record for this book is
available from the British Library.

ISBN-13: 978-1-4463-0142-5 paperback
ISBN-10: 1-4463-0142-7 paperback

Printed in China by RR Donnelley
for F&W Media International, LTD
Brunel House, Forde Close, Newton
Abbot, TQ12 4PU, UK

10 9 8 7 6 5 4 3 2 1

F+W Media Inc. publishes high-quality
books on a wide range of subjects.
For more great book ideas visit:
www.rucraft.co.uk

Contents

Preface 6

Getting Started 8

Selecting Fabrics 12

Machine-Made Quilts That Look Handmade . 14

Christmas Ideas..................... 22

Hearts on Squares..................... 27

Small Embroidery 29

Old Blocks, New Quilt 29

Tea-Towel Tote 34

Boy's Bag 35

Christmas Cushion 36

Summer Cushion 38

Pocket Pooch 39

Holiday Hearts Throw..................... 40

Waste-Not Wall Art 43

'Boy's Stuff' Quilt..................... 46

Shoulder Bag 50

Mini Purses 53

'Home is Best' Cushion 60

Doll's Quilt..................... 65

Alphabet Cushion 66

The Wheels on the Bus 68

Beautiful Borders 70

Hand-Sewn Coaster 74

Quick Key Ring 74

Simple Pincushions..................... 75

Button Mittens..................... 76

Button Bracelet..................... 77

Marbles Pouch 77

Pretty Pincushions 78

Needlework Jars 80

Pig Frame 82

Leftovers Cushion 85

Cute Sweater 86

Button Art 87

Denim Patch 88

Boy's Pyjamas 89

Angel Cushion 90

Appliqué Tea Towels 92

Pair of Potholders 95

'Many Hands' Memory Quilt 96

Heart Appliqué Instructions for Beginners..................... 99

Hearts Table Runner 100

Easter Table Topper 102

'Inspired by Anne' Pram Quilt..................... 103

Miniature Log Cabin Blocks..................... 105

Internet Stars Quilt..................... 108

Button Bag 110

Easter Tablecloth 112

Dedication 114

Suppliers..................... 114

Patterns..................... 116

Index 128

Preface

I was born with a brain that constantly makes associations and comes up with new ideas. These are scribbled down and filed in a folder. You can see some of these ideas as designs in this book – they were made over several years and in different stages. As I'm a very restless and impatient person, I soon get tired of struggling with one quilt and start thinking of ideas for new one. Therefore, I often start another project before I finish the first one, because that's a lot more fun to me. Later, and often much later, I go back to the unfinished one and complete it. The joy of seeing the quilt again gives me renewed energy to finish it. I hope you find some inspiration in this book, and, like me, you find a reason to have numerous half-finished projects in drawers and cupboards!

Trine

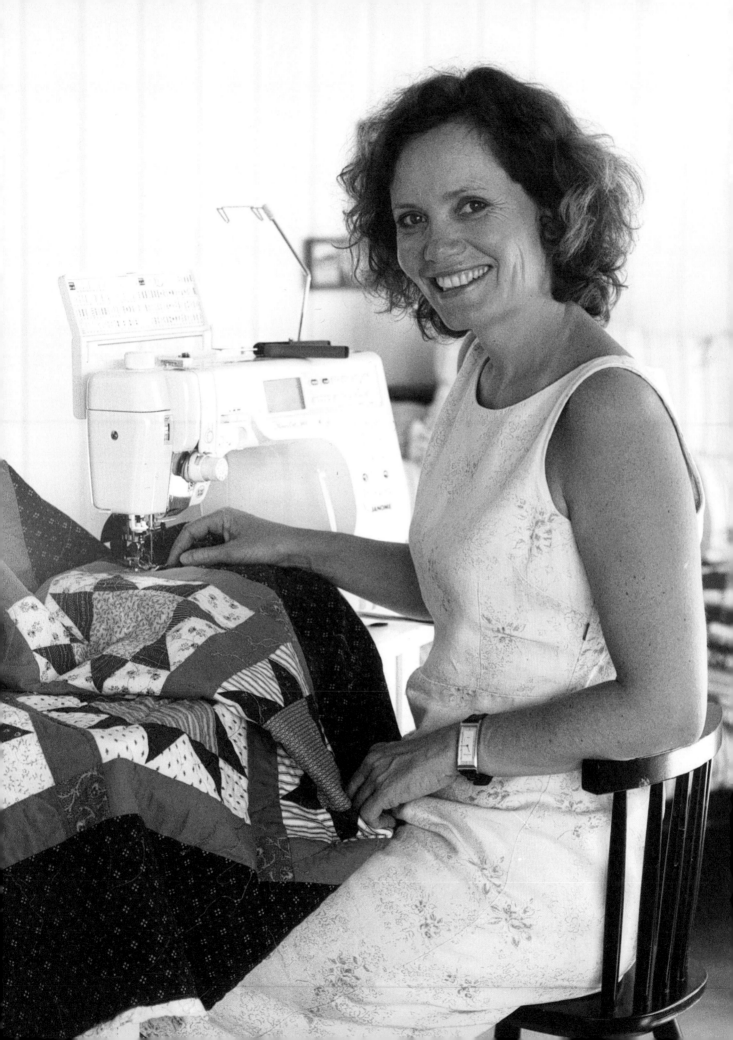

Getting Started

Fabric choice

All the designs in this book were made over several years with fabric from my own stash. Fabric collections change all the time and manufacturers rarely print the same collection twice. Therefore it will probably be very difficult to find the exact same fabrics as the ones illustrated in this book. This applies to most quilt books on the market.

If you find yourself struggling to find appropriate fabrics, pay a visit to your local haberdasher or quilt fabric supplier. Any good fabric supplier will help you to select fabrics that will work together for your project – take the book along with you and show them the quilt you have in mind to make, and I'm sure they will help you select the perfect fabrics that will work together to create the same impression as the designs illustrated here. If you do not have such resources on your doorstep, look in online shops for fat quarter bundles and jelly rolls that have been put together by experienced eyes and hands to give a selection of wonderful fabrics that work in perfect harmony with each other. I am sure you will make the right choices and will be delighted with the end results.

The sewing machine

Before you invest in a sewing machine, ask your friends that sew what they recommend and what features they think are the most important. When it comes to buying a sewing machine, always buy the very best you can afford – it's better to spend a little more money than you wanted and be absolutely delighted with your purchase than to go for a bargain machine and end up being disappointed with its lack of features.

For me, the following sewing machine features are essential:

- Dual feed for quilting
- Programmable needle up/down button which allows the needle to either finish in the up position or in the fabric
- Straight stitches with variable length
- Blanket stitches for machine appliqué
- Reminder to tell you when the bobbin is running out of thread
- Automatic thread cutter
- Lock stitch feature
- Knee lifter
- Adjustable straight stitch width to enable you to decide your seam allowance

Read before you sew

It's a good idea to read through the instructions before you start cutting and sewing. If you are lucky you can visualize the process, but if not you still have better odds of succeeding, as you subconsciously know what is going to happen next. I learned that it is helpful to have someone reading the instructions out loud while I fumble with the pieces. That way I can say, 'Wait, read that sentence again' – perhaps you will find this helps make the instructions clearer to you too.

In the front or back of most quilt books you will find good advice and guidance. This can be very useful to read and I have developed most of my technique by reading these pages thoroughly. Make it a habit always to read through the guidance and you will discover that there are often several ways of doing something. If you notice you come across the same problem over and over again, read everything you can find on the subject or join a class. Attending a class could give you great skills and knowledge.

Imperial or metric measurements?

I recommend all beginners to learn how to use inches. When you start out, you will be very dependent on quilt 'recipes' for step-by-step guidance. International books and patterns use inches (abbreviated to in or ") as a unit of measurement. Sewing machine feet that are specially made for patchwork and quilting are produced with a ¼in marking to help you to sew with this seam allowance. For this reason, I work with inches. I have used inches for years, my instructions are in inches and the people I sew with all use inches. All the designs in this book were made with inches and the instructions were written while sewing. The measurements are tried and tested and are most likely correct (although I am only human, and you should still allow for error).

The measurements in centimetres (cm) were calculated afterwards. I have not tried them out, therefore the chances of miscalculations in the metric measurements are greater. Instead of multiplying the inch number by 2.54 to get centimetres, I drew the blocks all over again to make it as accurate as possible. The seam allowance in centimetres is slightly larger than the seam allowance in inches, and this is reflected in the conversions given. But there is a chance that the finished product will differ from that shown if you use the metric rather than the imperial measurements. The designs in this book were sewn in inches, padded with cotton wadding (batting), shrunk by washing and then measured. Please take all of this into consideration when you choose what unit of measurement you want to use. Either way, I recommend that you sew the first few steps before you cut all the pieces needed. That's how I work.

Seam allowance for inches is ¼in.
Seam allowance for centimetres is 1cm.

Transfering patterns on a light table

A light table could be very helpful to you, but they do cost money. Alternatively you could use the method of taping the pattern to a window, then taping the fabric over this and using the sunshine as a natural light table.

You could also create a light table by putting two tables next to each other with some space between. Place a piece of glass over the gap and a lamp without the lampshade underneath.

You could also use your plexiglass quilt table instead of a piece of glass. Instead of a lamp you could use a drawing board lamp or similar that gives a lot of light but does not produce extreme heat.

Use water-soluble stabilizer if you plan to wash your work as soon as it is completed. This is a weave-like material that dissolves in water.

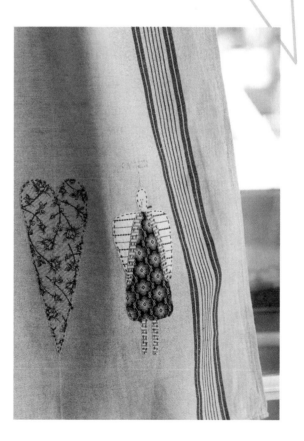

Be creative and spontaneous

I have worked in the same way for years and have held several classes to teach others how to work the way I do. To me, this gives me freedom and brings joy to the whole process. I rarely know what I am going to make before starting or where the project will fit in my house. I just start with some beautiful fabrics and sew a few blocks. When they are finished I decide if I should place them alternating, on point, maybe in strips, or perhaps a combination of everything. Then I find a filler, which is a fabric that should be used in whole pieces to bring something new in contrast to the blocks. After that I sew it all together so that I can figure out a border.

Even though the blocks are sewn at the same time they can be divided into several different projects with a completely different impression. I make fabric choices while I work, along with decisions on fillers, sashing, frames and how the border is going to work. This makes the process so much more fun as I love putting together different fabric combinations.

Choose a block and make plenty

It could be nine-patch blocks, four-patch blocks, pinwheels, churn dashes, puss in the corner, sawtooth star or blocks made using the log cabin technique.

A walk with the blocks

When I have finished the blocks I put them on a big tray and carry them around fabric shops or among my pieces of fabric at home, I call it 'a walk with the blocks'. The purpose is to look for nice fillers. Try to clear your brain and not have any preconceptions of what might look good or not. Suddenly you will see something that fits perfectly.

Nine-patch block *Four-patch block* *Pinwheels*

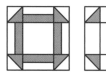

Different types of churn dashes *Puss in the corner*

  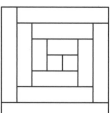

Sawtooth star *Log cabin block*

Fillers

In the photograph, right, the brown fabric is an example of what I call a filler. It is fabric used undivided, it is not supposed to be cut into pieces within the blocks. The blocks are already made with other fabrics. Use the filler fabric, cut in the same size as the sewn blocks, alternately with the blocks.

On point, alternating or stripes?

As shown below right, there are several ways to arrange the blocks. Use the filler in between.

Borders

When most of the quilt is finished, go for another walk with it. This time you walk around to find a border fabric. A border can consist of several rounds and different widths. There is no rule saying you need to have a thin border followed by a thicker one, it could also be the other way around.

Breaks

Sometimes the surface of your quilt could use some space. Use the filler as an extra border before you start the actual borders.

On point, in a stripe

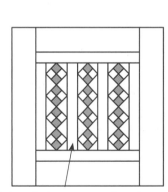

Stripes in between as breaks

On point

Horizontal

11

Selecting Fabrics

Start out with something and build on it. As an example, I start with a combination of orange and green, as in a carrot. Choose a few lighter fabrics and a few darker ones. Make sure the patterns vary so you have squares, flowers, dots and all-covering, and that the patterns are in different scales.

Expand your selection

Stretch the colour – this means that you could include more orange-looking colours. In this case I included violet, pink and ochre. I call all these colours a 'stretched orange'. I stretched the warm green colour to the cold and bright turquoise-green.

Try and stick to patterns that you think fit each other. None of the fabrics should stand out more than the others.The bright pink fabric is included to back up the strongest green colour. All the light fabrics are there to make it less compact because I want the finished product to be softer than just bright 'carrot' orange.

The fabrics shown to the right on page 13 are the leftover fabrics. Something about them did not work for me – they were either too sharp or too tame, had the wrong pattern or the wrong shade of the colour. To other people these fabrics could be perfect, but not for me. It's not science, just personal taste.

The photo above is how my finished collection looks. Some fabrics are later taken away and I am sure I will add some when I start to sew this together. I hide the combination in a box marked 'Soft Carrot'. Whenever I feel like sewing something I can take the box out and a lovely combination of fabrics are waiting for me. Another box I have saved from earlier is marked 'A Great Advent', and I am wondering right now if maybe the two boxes could be really good together?

Putting it all together

My Fabric Requirements

The following list sums up what I think about when I choose fabrics – it doesn't mean it's how you have to do it though.

1. Stretch the colours (see page 12).
2. Variation in patterns (squares, stripes, geometric patterns, flowers, dots, all-covering, repetition, mixed or clusters).
3. Variation from light to medium dark and dark in all colours.
4. Find fabrics that support the key fabrics – it will make them look less lonely.
5. Remove fabrics that steal all the attention.
6. Stick to one pattern family, but expand it. Only using flowers could be a little boring.
7. Divide the colours in percentages relative to what you want to achieve (especially if you are copying something).
8. Avoid using a whole collection from the same designer, the result might look very two-dimensional.
9. Don't use the same design in different colours. It will turn out looking boring.
10. Only pick patterns you like.
11. As long as you are happy with the pattern, you can choose colours you don't usually like that much.
12. Make a stand on the whiteness of fabrics and the purity of the patterns.
13. Make sure the moods of the fabrics fit each other.
14. Don't concentrate on different eras.

Start the selection of fabrics and let your intuition guide you, not the colour wheel.

Machine-Made Quilts That Look Handmade

I really like machine-made quilts, so the following text is probably not very objective. But what difference does it make when we are talking about quilts?

Handmade quilts are absolutely beautiful – whether they are sewn with large rough stitches or small perfect stitches. Work that is tightly padded by hand through thin quality cotton wadding (batting) is unbeatable, and it looks even prettier after it has been washed. The surface and structure becomes different than if you use synthetic wadding because cotton wadding can shrink. The stitches make hollows in the quilt that give it relief and shadow. Handmade quilt stitches go up and down and only cover parts of the seam line, while a machine seam covers all of the seam and leaves a sharper line.

I neither have the time nor the capacity to make all my quilts by hand, but a few of my quilts (none in this book) are handmade. I have experimented to work out how I can make a machine-made quilt look like it's handmade, especially at first glance and from a distance. A trained eye can see that I am using a machine to make quilts before an amateur can. If you want to try the same, here are a few things to bear in mind:

The quilt code

1. Have a thread audition
Spread out several different colours on the quilt. Use only a single thread, not the whole reel, as the colour is different when seen on the reel. Look for the colour that disappears more often. Dark colours are better than light. Light threads give contrast while dark gives shadow. Try out lots of colours, even colours that are not present in the quilt. Brown, gold, medium blue or olive often fit. Chose cotton, mercerized and a little thicker than regular sewing thread. I do not recommend waxed/lustrous hand quilt thread as it ruins the thread tension. Constantly change the colour of the thread so each patch of the quilt goes with the thread that disappears the most.

2. Use the same under thread as over thread
The thread underneath should be the same as the thread above. This way it doesn't matter if the thread tension is a little uneven, and you don't see the thread above or the thread underneath on the quilt top and/or backing. Make several bobbins for the under thread before you start. You will need more bobbins than you think for both over and under.

3. Choose a backing that hides your thread
Look at the photo on page 112 – this is a good camouflaging backing. The quilt is machine made with brown and yellow thread. A fabric with a large pattern with light and dark colours might have been even better though.

4. Use the quilting (even-feed) foot
As opposed to the standard presser foot or the freehand quilting (free-motion) foot. It will give you control and get the stitches even.

5. Use stitch length 4.5
The line you sew will look softer with longer stitches. Short stitches will give it a more compact look. Also, long stitches will look more handmade than short stitches from a distance. Loosen the thread tension and tighten the thread underneath. Sew a few tests.

6. Run into the ditch

Choose to sew 'in the ditch', meaning in the seam where there is no seam allowance. Illustrated above you can see a four-patch block machine sewn in the seam on the side where the seam allowance is not ironed, thus where there is already a natural 'ditch'. Sew as close to the seam as possible, without crossing over to the seam allowance. Some sewing machine manufacturers produce a great sewing machine foot that is made especially to do this. The stitches are continued along the middle of the border and around.

I often sew the whole quilt on machine 'in the ditch', and then later sew some stitches with a seam allowance distance (¼in or 1cm) from a few seams to highlight shapes.

7. Follow the squares and stripes

When you have used a fabric with a square or striped pattern, you can follow the pattern when you sew on the machine. Chose a colour that fits and place yourself in the transition between a stripe and another colour. This way you don't have to mark up. When I do need to make markings I use tailor's chalk or a pencil.

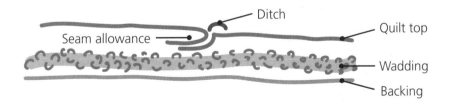

Ditch

Seam allowance

Quilt top

Wadding

Backing

Diagonals, lattice or close parallel stripes are among my favourites. They are easy to mark up and easy to follow.

8. Complicated patterns on small quilts

The pattern with the heart and feather wreath shown on page 17 is machine made with the quilting foot. Since you constantly have to flip and turn the quilt around, this type of pattern is best suited to baby blankets, table runners and table toppers. The pattern is transferred with pencil using a plastic quilting stencil.

9. Use a straight needle in the machine

Use a size 80 or 90 quilting needle with a tapered point. Change it frequently, preferably every fourth hour. Consult your machine's user manual and use the needles they recommend.

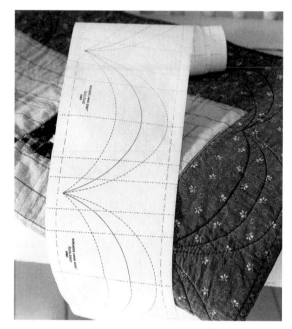

10. Use adhesive tear-away border patterns

This paper aid (pictured above right) has sticky edges and the ability to adjust the length. The stitching pattern is pre-printed. Tear away the paper after quilting. This is a boring job with a lot of paper waste, so I place myself in front of the TV with a rubbish bin nearby. The stitches

will stretch a little bit when you remove the paper. If they go completely out of shape you can adjust them back with a needle. Or the easiest alternative is to wash the quilt when you are finished, then the threads will adjust by themselves.

Using this method it is possible to make attractive arcs and angles without too much practice. Stop the needle where the angle changes. Make the arc in one motion. It's easier to turn the quilt around in the machine if you put these at the edge of the quilt.

You will find a number of patterns for different borders in different sizes and a few central section patterns among the commercially available products. You don't need to mark up or use stencils. One roll can be used for several quilts if you copy the corners. The paper has a strong tape that attaches along the edge and that can be moved. The paper is docile and you can curl it and turn it around in the machine. Use straight stitches and the quilting foot.

Start by placing the corners. Measure a length and remember that the start up from the corner has to be right. Take more or less paper, depending on whatever gives the lowest difference. Cut it along the marks and overlap or pull apart. Follow the markings and sew around the quilt. Remember to lift your hand in the turns while the needle is down.

11. Proper tacking is important
Use spray adhesive, hand tacking, tacking gun or pins. I prefer spray adhesive. The layers have to be attached well and without creases. Unfortunately, problems will not disappear during quilting. It will actually stand out if the fabrics don't lie properly.

12. Clean the table and roll the quilt
You need space in order to get the quilt into the machine. Choose a smooth table over a raw pine one. Roll the quilt tightly so it can fit in the opening between the needle and the body of the sewing machine. Throw the roll over your shoulder, steer and lift the roll forwards. The feed dogs can't pull a heavy quilt, so you have to make sure nothing prevents its progress while you push the quilt lightly forwards. Some machines have more room than others.

13. Find a way to secure the threads
Hold the ends of the thread, sew approximately ⅛in (5mm) with 0.5 stitch length. Stop and set the running stitch to 4.5. Quilt and then stop ⅛in (5mm) away from where you plan to secure the thread. Lower the stitch length again and sew ⅛in (5mm) with 0.5 stitch length. Pull the upper thread to the back side with the thread underneath. Both threads should now be secured by hand from the back side, or you can tie them together and cut or just cut them away. The last two methods described can lead

to the threads becoming loose over time. I usually just cut the ends. Thread trouble occurs when the thread is not tight at the beginning. If the quilt is big, it can be difficult. In this case, try to leave the last seam so it tightens over the thread. Secure and then cut away the tightening. The camouflage fabric on the backing can hide a few 'disasters'.

You can secure threads the usual way by sewing a little back and forth if the wadding (batting) seam goes from outer edge to outer edge. This will be hidden under the border anyway.

14. Wash the quilt when it's finished
Shrinking and creases give a hand-quilted, antique look to it.

This method of machine quilting is different to freehand quilting with the machine. Not only because I choose the thread after the fabric and change it often, but also because the stitches rarely cross an element. I have tried to pass on my preferences in quilting, and I hope that now you are capable of finding your own, if you don't already have them.

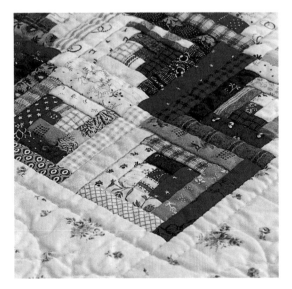

How do I work out the right length for the borders?

I consistently only list the width of borders. You find the length like this: when you get as far as putting on the borders, stop and iron the quilt top. Take the border strips and place them parallel with the edge – in the centre of the quilt – and cut them to match the length.

Cut two edges at the same time by placing them on top of each other. Make marks on the borders and quilt, pin the edges and sew them on. Iron and do the same for the next two borders. I always sew on the borders on the long sides first. I think this makes the quilt more harmonious, but that's just my opinion.

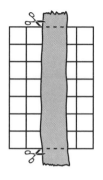

Measure with the strip in the middle of the piece. Cut the right length.

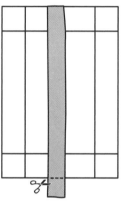

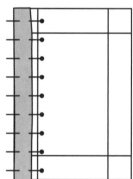

Pin the outer edge and sew it on. Iron and repeat for the other edge.

Christmas Ideas

I always look for photo frames, albums or other things I can decorate with fabric. Here, I have bought some books with apertures intended for photos on the cover. Of course, I glue fabrics in the apertures instead. The book has a loose paper page that I glue behind the aperture after attaching the fabric with a glue stick. A small three-patch block that was leftover from some patchwork was roughly appliquéd onto a white piece of wool fabric and inserted into a square aperture. I used visible knots and tacking stitches in brown embroidery thread. For interest, I added a couple of cross stitches.

You can give the books as gifts or use them yourself for Christmas check lists. Who got what presents? What year? What did you get?

Who will be where on Christmas Eve this year? Where were we on Christmas Day last year? What's the menu? Who will get Christmas cards? Write in all the addresses for Christmas cards. When do we have to send the Christmas gifts up north?

The matchboxes, pictured below, are dressed with wool felt. You can glue this on with a glue stick or glue gun. Or you could use fusible web and iron it on, as you do for appliqué. The bow is folded and glued on. Buttons and ribbons are also just glued on. Place the felt around three sides leaving one side where you can light the matches. This makes it easier to make the fabric neat and it feels more solid when it goes all around. Another trick is to make the felt very

slightly smaller than the box on all sides. This way the felt is more solidly attached to the box.

It's a real advantage to use a glue gun. The glue dries fast and it's fairly solid. But be careful with your fingers – this is very hot stuff! From time to time repairs with the glue gun will be necessary. I keep my glue gun in a nice roomy box. The box is on my book shelf. Every time something needs to be fixed I just place it in the box. Next time I am using the glue gun I fix whatever needs to be fixed at the same time.

The candle decoration, shown right, is made with cotton thread. Shape the ribbon into a circle. Fold in an overlapping hem and glue it together with the glue gun. The button is first decorated with a piece of thread and then the whole button is glued to the ribbon with the glue gun. Make the circle a little loose so it can easily be removed from the candle. Make sure you remove the decoration before the candle burns all the way down.

The little wall decoration, pictured left, is made for a hanger that exists in several sizes. This one measures 5½in (14cm) wide. Cut out a piece of red wool felt measuring 8¼ x 4½in (21 x 11.5cm). Fold the fabric around the hanger and glue with the glue gun so the length becomes 5½in (14cm). Alternatively you can make a tacking seam across. Attach the buttons randomly or in a harmonious pattern with embroidery thread or a glue gun.

Hearts on Squares

Size: approximately 23½ x 27in (60 x 69.5cm)

This quilt was sewn for a friend when she finally understood the rules of my favourite card game. The colours were chosen to fit the Advent time before Christmas. I'm not a big fan of the traditional Advent purple, so I have tried to stretch the colour towards golden.

Christmas calendar

If you sew on buttons to the quilt, you can make this a Christmas calendar with little presents hanging on it. I usually number the presents and put them in a basket. Next to the basket I arrange the quilt randomly.

You will need:

- 25 background fabrics, 4 x 4¾in (10 x 12cm)
- 25 heart fabrics, 4 x 4in (10 x 10cm)
- Fabric for the inner border, 3in (8cm)
- Fabric for the central border, 5½in (14cm)
- Fabric for the outer border, 2½in (6cm)
- Backing fabric, 27½ x 31½in (70 x 80cm)
- Wadding (batting), 27½ x 31½in (70 x 80cm)
- Machine/hand embroidery thread
- Fusible web
- Tear-away stabilizer (or paper towels)

Choice of colours and patterns

This quilt is made in purple, violet, golden brown, red, orange and old rose colours.

The fabric patterns are checked and other geometric patterns. The border has a discreet flower pattern.

Instructions:

Cut the 25 pieces of background fabric to size, 4 x 4¾in (10 x 12cm). Choose both bright and dark colours. Choose 25 fabrics for the heart appliqués. There should be enough contrast so you can see the heart from a distance, but vary the degree of contrast. Let a few hearts be very clear and others more diffused. Also vary the patterns on the fabrics.

Machine appliqué

Place fusible web on top of the heart template and trace on the paper side with a pencil. Draw 25 hearts and cut them out. Iron the appliqué film to the reverse side of the heart fabrics. Notice that some of my hearts are slightly tilted in the square. All the backgrounds are angular in the squares and the hearts are mostly tilted at different subtle angles. Cut out along the pencil line. Peel off the paper and iron the heart to the background fabric.

Put tear-away stabilizer (or paper towels) behind the squares down towards the machine. Some sewing machines have decorative stitches and some can look like handmade buttonhole stitch, so experiment with the sewing machine and sew a test patch first. Measure the length and width of the stitch so it fits the size of the heart.

Hand appliqué

To do it by hand is the same as described above except the final part. Sew around the hearts with hand stitches with two strands of embroidery thread and appliqué stitches.

Sewing it together

Lay the hearts out in rows of five. Decide on the final placement after trying out different combinations. Pin a little piece of paper to each heart so you know the sequence when you are sewing. Iron the seam allowance alternately towards the left and right like this: row 1, 3 and 5 to the left and row 2 and 4 to the right. Sew the rows together. Use pins so the rows don't move. The seam allowance is ironed alternate ways to ease the adjustment.

Borders

The inner border is cut 1½in (4cm). The outer border is cut 2½in (6.5cm).

Wadding (batting)

Place the backing, wadding and the quilt top on top of each other and tack them all together by hand. You can also use temporary fabric adhesive.

Every square is quilted a seam allowance distance from all seams. It will turn out just as well if you quilt down into all the seams (see page 17) and around the hearts.

Attach the border, sew on a hanger and make a tag to appliqué behind the quilt.

The pattern is on page 123.

28

Small Embroidery

Remove the glass in the frame. Taking inspiration from the shape of the aperture, tack a pattern freehand onto white woolen fabric, glue onto a piece of card and attach to the back plate of the frame with tape.

Old Blocks, New Quilt (see page 31)

This little quilt says a lot about how I work. I sewed these star blocks in the early 1990s, put them in a draw and forgot about them! They are now put together with new elements. I always save spare blocks as they can often come to use in other projects. Here, six stars are attached with lattice work and corner blocks before I added two borders. To me, the red broad outer border is the most important part of this quilt. The other pieces almost just lie around to make this fabric shine. Broad frames in beautiful fabrics are an element brought from old Scandinavian quilts. The small four-patch block that creates the corner blocks of the lattice work are leftovers from the quilt pictured on page 47. The bright white in the frame is repeated in some of the light fabrics in the four-patch blocks. The greys in the old stars are reflected in the checked narrow outer border.

Size: approximately 28¼ x 35in (72 x 89cm) after washing and shrinkage.

You will need:
- Six pieces of fabric (blue, turquoise, green, red) for the centre of the stars, 4 x 4in (10 x 10cm)
- Six pieces of fabric (purple, red, blue and brown) for the star points, 14 x 4in (35 x 10cm)
- Six pieces of fabric (blue, beige, golden, red and purple) for the star background, 20 x 4in (50 x 10cm)
- 12 pieces of light fabric for the four-patch blocks, 4 x 4in (10 x 10cm)
- 12 pieces of dark fabric (black, grey, olive, blue) for the four-patch blocks, 4 x 4in (10 x 10cm)
- Tender green fabric for the lattice work sashing, 14in (35cm)
- Blue checked fabric for the inner border, 12in (30cm)

5 x 5in (12 x 12cm)

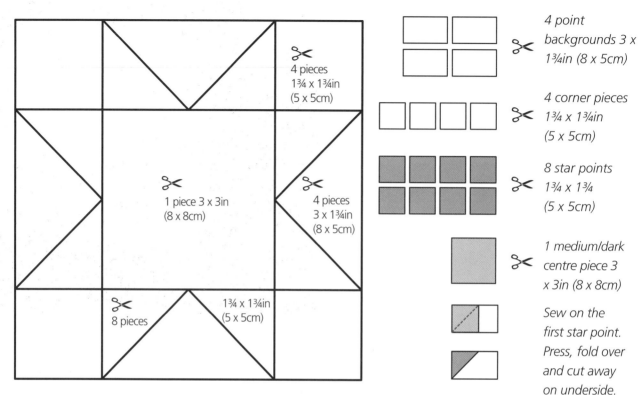

4 pieces
1¾ x 1¾in
(5 x 5cm)

1 piece 3 x 3in
(8 x 8cm)

4 pieces
3 x 1¾in
(8 x 5cm)

8 pieces

1¾ x 1¾in
(5 x 5cm)

4 point
backgrounds 3 x
1¾in (8 x 5cm)

4 corner pieces
1¾ x 1¾in
(5 x 5cm)

8 star points
1¾ x 1¾
(5 x 5cm)

1 medium/dark
centre piece 3
x 3in (8 x 8cm)

Sew on the
first star point.
Press, fold over
and cut away
on underside.
Sew on the
next star point

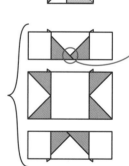

¼in (1cm) seam
allowance.
The seams of
the star points
will make an X

Trim the
blocks
to size

- Red/white large-scale patterned fabric for the large border,
28in (70cm)
- Grey-brown checked fabric for the outer border, 14in (35cm)
- Backing fabric, 40 x 45in (100 x 115cm)
- Cotton wadding (batting), 40 x 45in (100 x 115cm)

Making the star blocks

For each star block (see diagram above) cut:
- One dark/medium dark square for the centre, 3 x 3in (8 x 8cm)
- Eight dark squares for the star points, 1¾ x 1¾in (5 x 5cm)
- Four light squares for the background corners, 1¾ x 1¾in
(5 x 5cm)
- Four light rectangles for the background points, 3 x 1¾in
(8 x 5cm)

Sew the cut pieces together with a ¼in (1cm) seam allowance,
following the diagrams, right.

Making the four-patch blocks

- Cut 24 light and 24 dark pieces from the 12 light and 12 dark
fabrics, each piece measuring 1⅝ x 1⅝in (4.75 x 4.75cm).
Sew 12 blocks of four from the total of 48 pieces.

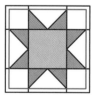

1⅝ x 1⅝in
(4.75 x 4.75cm)

Four-patch blocks

Further cutting:
• Cut 17 rectangles in light green for the lattice work, measuring 2¾ x 5½in (7.5 x 14cm)
• Cut the checked border, 2¾in (7.5cm) wide.
• Cut the flower pattern for the wide border, 4¾in (13cm) wide.

The backing is just as important as the front. Quilts are lifted, folded and turned around and the backing will show. It is suppose to be beautiful and work as a camouflage for the quilting done on the sewing machine and for thread knots. I piece my backings randomly but make sure they are in harmony. Even if a quilt is designed to hang on the wall, it can suddenly get a new life after 15 years, for example through inheritance, redecorating or moving. Then it's important that the backing looks good.

The outer border (binding) is 2¼in (6cm) wide and is attached in a strip that is folded lengthways with the right side out. Sew the border from the right side edge against edge. Finally sew the border by hand to the backing.

The tag is written with a textile marker on the backing. The quilting is done over the tag and kind of works like a security system; to remove the tag the quilting needs to be removed and the backing needs to be pieced all over again.

All seams of the quilt are machine quilted. Also, quilting is sewn a seam allowance distance from the edges of the long sides in the lattice work and around the central piece of each star. The checked border is quilted with two lines that follow the check. In addition, I used an adhesive tear-away border design on the outer border.

Notice the machine quilting – the stitch length is 4.5 using normal, thin cotton thread. Use the same colour and quality in both the bobbin and the over thread. I change thread all the time and choose a colour that either disappears or makes a shadow (see page 14).

Tea-Towel Tote

From tea towel to tote bag in less than half an hour! This bag be used as a shopping bag, beach bag or as a rainwear bag for kids in nursery school. Hang a few on pegs in your hallway so you will always have one to hand.

You will need:
• A tea towel, approximately 20 x 27½in (50 x 70cm). Choose one that is nicely folded from the factory
• 4 nice buttons
• 14in (36cm) cotton ribbon, linen ribbon or similar for four loops x 3½in (9cm)
• Two ready-made plastic bag handles, or two strong ribbons, 30in (75cm) each folded in nicely at each end

Instructions:
Use a strong thread and strong sewing machine needle (for example, jeans size 90). This might require you to adjust the thread tension. Try a test piece first – something you should do before starting any project.

Attach a handle on each short end of the towel. Use a ribbon or a ready-made handle and cover the seam with a button. I used a cotton ribbon and threaded the handle through.

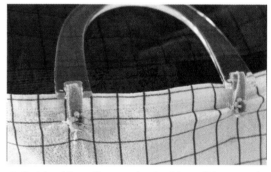

With nothing in them, these bags fold up really small like plastic bags, the difference is that these are more beautiful and eco-friendly.

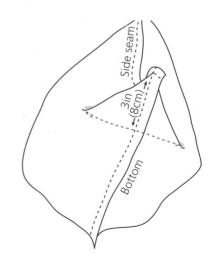

A finished handle attached with a ribbon and a button to a tea towel. And hey presto – you have a bag!

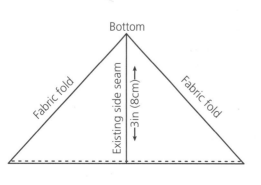

Fold the towel so the right side is facing inwards and the handles are lying on top of each other. Sew the side seams and secure the thread well at the beginning and end. Fold a false bottom in each side and sew across. Make sure the angle of the seam is 45 degrees on the fold and 90 degrees on the side seam. It can be a good idea to make a cardboard template if you are making several false bottoms. See illustration opposite.
Cut away the ugly washing instructions and the loop.

Boy's Bag

Porcelain car buttons set the theme for this tea-towel bag, made in the same way. It can be used back and forth to nursery school with a change of clothes. I have it hanging in the hallway and I fill it up as I remember what I need to take to the nursery. The bag can also be kept at school containing spare clothing in case of spills or extra layers if the weather changes.

Christmas Cushion

Size: approximately 17½ x 17½in (44 x 44cm) after washing and shrinkage.

Simple squares in brown and red framed with corner squares makes the 'Christmassy' front of this cushion. The reverse side (see page 38) is put together from another fabric and an old shirt. The back of the cushion has lighter colours and is used on the sofa in the summer.

You will need:
• 20 different pieces of fabric in brown and red for the front side, 6 x 6in (15 x 15cm)
• Brown fabric with checked pattern for the borders, 6in (15cm)
• Cotton wadding (batting), 20 x 20in (50 x 50cm)
• An old shirt for the back panel along with

a suitable summery fabric to piece with so that the back panel measures 20 x 20in (50 x 50cm) (the same size as the front side when it is finished).

Instructions:
Sew together the front side of the cushion following the diagram below. Put wadding (batting) behind it and tack the wadding to the front side. You can also use temporary fabric adhesive. The cushion is quilted a seam allowance distance from each seam. Sew one line south and one line east on the squares, not around all sides. The border has two lines of quilting that follow the check. The corners are quilted along the seams towards the border.

See Summer Cushion on next page.

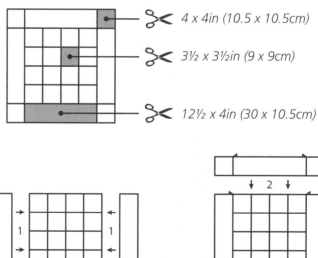

4 x 4in (10.5 x 10.5cm)

3½ x 3½in (9 x 9cm)

12½ x 4in (30 x 10.5cm)

Piecing diagrams with ironing guide

Summer Cushion

This is the reverse side of the Christmas Cushion shown on page 37. Find an old shirt that is not in use anymore. It can be out of use because the collar or cuffs are worn, because it's out of fashion or because it doesn't fit anymore. Visit a flea market if you can't find any in your own wardrobe. I usually save shirts like this in a box because I know they will come to use one day. Choose a shirt you think fits as a summer cushion. The benefit of using a shirt instead of regular fabric is that the closing mechanism is already finished from the factory. In my opinion a cushion cover should be removable so you can clean it. To put in a zip is a bit of a struggle, so this way you can avoid doing that.

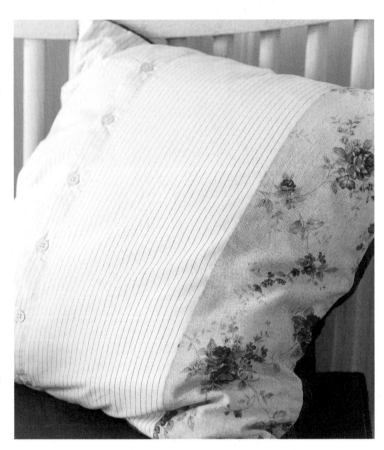

If the shirt front is too small (as they often are), use as much as you can of the button section and add an extra piece of fabric that contrasts with the shirt. This rose fabric works brilliantly with the striped shirt.

Instructions:

Iron the shirt front. Put the shirt right side to right side on top of the cushion front. Make sure the opening is horizontal and that no buttons are in the way of the sewing machine. Pockets and tags are interesting accessories that can stay. Read the text below the photograph if the shirt front is smaller than the size needed. Pin, sew all around the edge and cut the excess fabric away.

Clip the corners, open the buttons and turn right side out. Wash the cushion cover once, then press and insert a soft inner cushion of the correct size.

Tips

• If you are a beginner, avoid using a squared fabric in the outer edge as it can be very hard to make it even.

• Making cushions from shirts is perfect if you are working with children. It's easy to do and the cushion will be completed quickly!

Pocket Pooch

A jacket with an ugly pocket emblem is transformed into a beautiful blazer with a dog appliqué. I chose neutral and low contrast colors so the boy look stylish and not to show off mummy's sewing skills!

Instructions:

Take a square of appropriately sized fabric and iron fusible web to the reverse side. Trace the dog template on another piece of fusible web. Use a photocopier to enlarge or reduce the design if necessary. Cut it out roughly. Iron onto the wrong side of the dog fabric. Cut it out precisely. Remove the paper and iron against the square. Remove the paper on the square under the fusible web. Don't iron further at this time. Appliqué the dog with tacking stitches. Then iron the square with the appliqué dog to the blazer pocket. Appliqué the patch with tacking stitches, being careful not to sew the pocket and blazer together.

The pattern is on page 116.

Appliqué done with tacking stitches is less hard wearing than using zigzag stitch on the sewing machine. The appliqué will get a little loose around the edges after washing, but I find this more charming than annoying.

Holiday Hearts Throw

Size: approximately 37¾ x 52½in (96 x 133cm)

I usually prepare a little sewing bag before holidays, in which I put patterns and equipment so I can entertain the woman and children wherever I'm going (the men are usually a little harder to motivate!). Suitable projects are sewing over cardboard and appliqué on ready-made wool blankets or neutral tea towels.

My experience is that when I start my needlework, people around me want to help. So that I don't have to hand out parts of my own work, I have the sewing bag for family and friends to use. I pack some pieces of fabric, embroidery needles, threads, scissors and a travel iron. And most importantly, bring ready-edged wool blankets. Alternatively, you can cut out a blanket in the size you want and edge it yourself using appliqué stitches.

My family and friends contributed to this pretty throw during the Easter break. I washed the blanket on the wool programme in my washing machine before we appliquéd on it. We cut out the patterns for the hearts from newspaper.

Draw 12 hearts on fusible web and cut them out roughly. Iron against the wrong side of the heart fabrics. Remove the paper and iron all the hearts to the blanket. Be careful with the hot iron, as wool does not tolerate strong heat.

Appliqué around all the hearts. This is something everybody in the family can do, at least from age five and up. Let the kids participate and help out if they want to. You will find appliqué instructions for beginners on page 99.

I think it looks best to use thread in the same colour as the blanket, since the blanket is not padded. This way the stitches will not show too much on the reverse side. On the other hand, if the person stitching is not happy about the quality of their stitches, a colour that matches the heart could be better to camouflage the poor stitching.

We sewed two throws this Easter, but only one is shown here. This blanket was made by Hilde. Thank you for lending it to me and thank you for a nice holiday.

The pattern is on page 117.

Waste-Not Wall Art

There are always leftovers from quilting – different strips in different widths – and I collect them all in a basket. Some of them end up as wall art pieces. In this case I used a neutral strip for the centre section and sewed borders around it. The border pieces can be the same or different and even have different widths. It all depends on what you find in your leftovers basket. I placed the centre piece with borders on the photocopier and then sketched on the paper to find a suitable line drawing for the centre. The size of the motif must be in keeping with the size of the fabric pieces.

Heart tree (see opposite)
Size: approximately 6¼ x 4½in (16 x 11cm)

You will need:
• Centre piece: 1⅞ x 4¼in (5.5 x 11.75cm)
• Bottom border piece: 1½in (4.5cm)
• Three other border pieces: 1¾in (5.5cm)
• Wool or silk thread for machine embroidery or embroidery thread for hand embroidery

Friendly farmer (see page 44)
Size: approximately 6¼ x 3¾in (16 x 9.5cm)

You will need:
• Centre piece 1⅞ x 4½in (5.5 x 12cm)
• Top border: 1¾in (5.5cm)
• Three other border pieces: 1⅝ (5cm)

Embroidering the motif
Transfer the line drawing with the help of a light table (see page 9) onto the centre piece of fabric with a pencil. The pencil line will most likely stay on the fabric, so draw carefully. Alternatively, use water-soluble stabilizer. This makes it easy but it does require you to wash or moisten the fabric afterwards to remove the stabilizer. Draw the design on the stabilizer and pin it over the area that will be embroidered. Then embroider and finish the wall art. When you have finished, wash the fabric to remove the stabilizer.

You can embroider by hand with embroidery thread or on a sewing machine with wool or silk thread. Place wadding (batting) behind the fabric on which you have drawn the motif. Sew on top of the pencil line with embroidery stitches. If you are using a sewing machine, sew with running stitch/three-step running stitch. You have to lift the foot and turn often. Keep the needle in the fabric to turn more easily without breaking the line. With a machine you can easily sew through both layers.

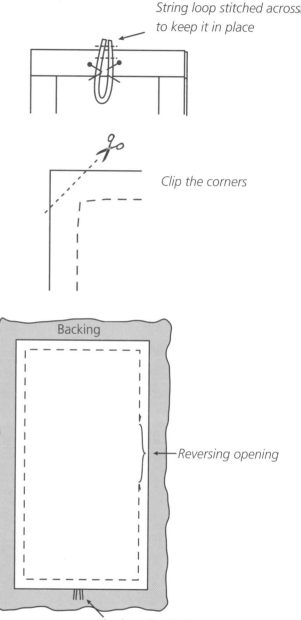

String loop stitched across to keep it in place

Clip the corners

Backing

Reversing opening

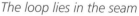

The loop lies in the seam

If you want to do the embroidery by hand you will find it can be hard to get through the wadding (batting). It can be a good idea to embroider through the fabric only and add the wadding later. Or, choose a thin cotton wadding and sew through both layers.

Most sewing machines have a strengthened running stitch. This is very well suited for embroidery. Use the sewing machine as you do for regular stitching, not freehand. I prefer this method because I have better control over the stitches, thread tension and, not least, the design. The result will look just as though I have drawn it. I allow some deviation from the drawing 'accidentally on purpose'. This method of embroidery requires that the work is not too big since you have to turn it around all the time for the stitches to be in the right place. Always stop with the needle down in the fabric and count the stitches so you know if the sewing machine is going to take a step forwards or backwards on the next stitch.

Use the clear presser foot. This way it is easier to see where you should turn to follow the pencil stroke. Try out different stitches on your machine, you find many new ones in the instruction manual. Or you can sew by hand. If you don't want to embroider, you can sew on some decorative buttons instead, such as the farmer button I have used. I have two big jars full of exciting buttons that I have collected from long before I started making quilts.

Make a string loop before you sew the wall art. Cut a loop approximately 3–4in (8–10cm) long and place it flat and folded double. Sew a couple of stitches across the ends so they stay in place. Attach the loop with tacking stitches or pins in the middle of the upper edge of the front side with the loop pointing downwards (see diagram opposite). If you don't want the wall art to tilt inwards after hanging it on the wall, be sure to make two loops.

I usually attach wadding (batting) and the front side with spray adhesive, but tacking is also a good alternative.

The wadding (batting) and the front piece are now on top of each other and should be cut to size. When you come to sew the edges on the reverse side and then the backing to the front piece/wadding later, you will need a clean line on the front piece to attach it properly. Therefore, neatly cut the front piece/wadding to the right size including the seam allowance. Cut from the side where you can see the front piece and measure it carefully so that the edges are properly straight and the borders are even and wide enough to allow for the seam.

Place the backing fabric right side to right side with the front piece. The wadding (batting) is already attached to the front piece. Place the wadding side facing you and sew the edges together on the reverse side around the whole piece, leaving an opening to turn it right side out. Secure the stitches tightly at the beginning and end of the stitching line and also sew a little back and forth over the string loop.

Cut away the fabric and wadding (batting) from the corners, and trim the wadding along the sides. Turn the wall art right side out, pushing out the corners so that they become as perpendicular as possible. Tuck the seam allowance into the reversing opening and press the whole piece. Close the gap by hand with invisible stitches.

Use quilt stitches or appliqué stitches for the edge of the border. I used a felt stitch, set wider than the normal setting on the sewing machine. I chose this particular backing fabric to camouflage the stitches on the reverse.

I sewed on buttons in each corner to balance the composition at the very end, after sewing on the backing and doing the quilting. In the absence of buttons you can use appliqué or embroider the outline of a button.

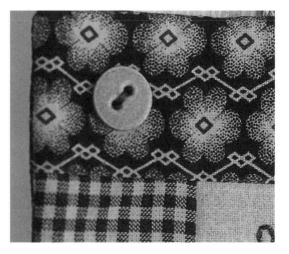

'Boy's Stuff' Quilt

Size: approximately 70 x 46in (175 x 116cm) after washing and shrinkage.

I am lucky enough to have had two girls, then to have another child, this time a boy. I was very excited to sew 'boy's stuff' for the first time. This usually happens the other way round, when mothers have only boys, then have a girl they can dress up in pink. But since I had already dressed up my girls for 13 years, the craving for pink wasn't really there anymore. Cars and trains on the other hand really gave me new motivation to continue quilting with a masculine theme. This quilt was made a while after I started with the 'boy's stuff'. I have chosen cute baby fabrics with dogs and cats and also fabrics with numbers and playing children. The cute baby fabrics are toned down with rough masculine fabrics. This block is easy to make and is called 'puss in the corner'.

You will need:
• Blue fabric for the border, 47¼in (120cm)
• Beige checked fabric for the filler squares and inner border, 51in (130cm)
• Up to 69 different fabrics in light, medium and dark for the blocks. I used some of the fabrics more than once, so I didn't have 69 different ones. One piece 8 x 6in (20 x 15cm) is enough
• Thick compact wadding (batting), queen size
• Backing fabric, approximately 80 x 55in (200 x 140cm)

Cutting list:
• Cut 22 filler squares in beige checked fabric, 6¾ x 6¾in (18 x 18cm)
• Cut the beige inner border, 3in (7.5cm)
• Cut the blue border, 6in (15cm)

• Cut 12 light squares for the blocks, 4½ x 4½in (12 x 12cm)
• Cut 48 light corners for the blocks, 1⅝ x 1⅝in (5 x 5cm)
• Cut 11 dark squares for the blocks, 4½ x 4½in (12 x 12cm)
• Cut 44 dark corners for the blocks, 1⅝ x 1⅝in (5 x 5cm)
• Cut 92 rectangles for the blocks, 4½ x 1⅝in (12 x 5cm)
This is a total of 23 puss in the corner blocks, 12 light and 11 dark.

Notice that the outer blocks have dark borders and the blocks in the middle have light borders.

Sew together the blocks and filler squares in rows of five, with every other row starting with a sewn block.

The quilt is quilted in all seams. I used an adhesive tear-away border pattern on the outer border. This is a paper quilting aid which you quilt on top of and tear away when you are finished (see page 18).

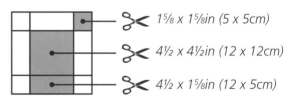

✄ 1⅝ x 1⅝in (5 x 5cm)

✄ 4½ x 4½in (12 x 12cm)

✄ 4½ x 1⅝in (12 x 5cm)

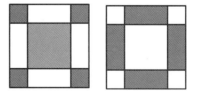

There are two different placements of lights and darks in the blocks

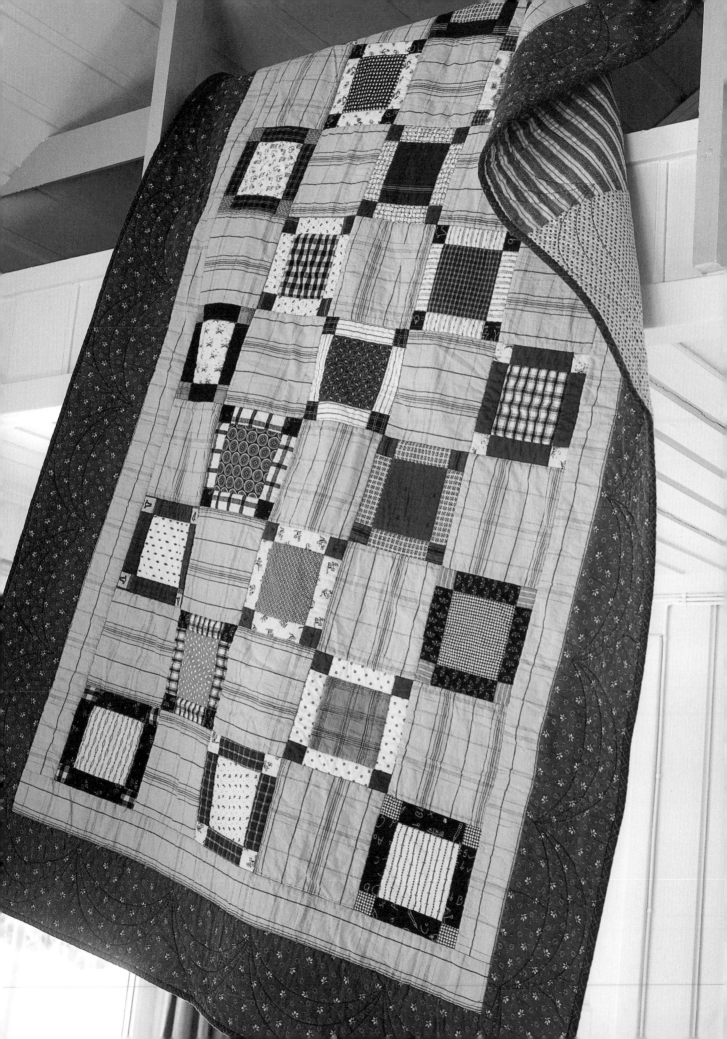

I originally planned the black fabric with the numbers on it for the whole quilt. I usually don't use black and especially when there is a bright white contrast in the pattern, but I found it so charming I just had to include it. It then became important for me to tone down the black and the contrasts. I did that using olive, beige, grey, brown, blue and dark turquoise-blue and also black and white fabrics. Choose masculine fabrics, and by that I mean anything that is not feminine. Feminine is flowers and pink, I especially tried to avoid flowers. Only humorous or very graphic flowers were allowed to join. Squares, stripes, geometrical patterns and dots are masculine patterns. Childish boyish fabrics that are not too cute are also nice to use. These requirements exclude a large portion of available fabrics, therefore you need to be creative and collect fabrics over time.

You don't have to place your quilts on beds or on the wall. They can work as decorations folded in nice piles.

Shoulder Bag

I have saved this fabric for a long time, it's an old favourite. In this bag the zip and handles are sewn on at an early stage. The final machine seams are sewn inside the bag, in the side seams and the bottom. There is some sewing to be done by hand when the strap is attached.

You will need:
• Zip, 8in (20cm)
• Black checked fabric, 16in (40cm)
• Wadding (batting), 16in (40cm)
• Lining fabric, 12in (30cm)

Cutting list:
• Cut 4 x 41½in (10 x 105cm) fabric and 1 x 41½in (2.5 x 105cm) wadding (batting) for the strap
• Cut two pieces for the exterior measuring 12¼in (31cm) wide x 9½in (25cm) high. Take a couple of minutes to figure out the width and height in relation to the direction of the pattern
• Cut two pieces of wadding and two pieces of lining the same size as the exterior

Instructions:
Begin with the strap. Fold the fabric wrong sides together lengthways, fold in a ½in (1.5cm) hem along the whole strap and iron in place. Place the wadding (batting) on the reverse of the fabric. Wrap the wadding with the fabric so the hem on one side covers the cut edge the other side. Pin lengthways and sew three lines of stitching all the way along so the hem is captured in the seam (see diagrams below).

Make two separate sides of the bag. Place the fabric and lining right sides together with the wadding (batting) on top. Include the strap in the seam on one of the sides, (1in) 3cm from each outer edge. Sew a seam across the top of the pieces. Fold out so you have a sandwich with padding in between which is nicely sewn together on one side, with the strap sticking out at the top. Make the other side in the exact same way, but without the strap. Change to the zipper foot and sew on the zip with

one line of stitching all the way down the zip, a seam allowance distance from the edge. As well as attaching the zip, the stitching also gives a decorative edge around the zip, allowing the inside of the bag

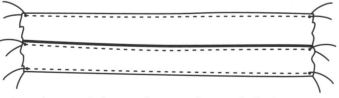

Lengthways stitches on the strap that catch the hem

Side view of the strap folds

to show a little bit. Sew the zip to one side at a time. The two separate parts have now become one piece with a zip in between.

The photos on page 50 show how the fabrics are placed around the wadding (batting) and how the zip is sewn. These photos show the making of a toiletries bag. It does not have a strap, but shows you how to sew on the zip before you do any further work.

Fold the bag so both of the outsides are lying right side to right side. Open the zip enough to reverse it later. Change back to the regular foot. Sew the side seams and bottom. Sew over the seams with a close zigzag stitch.

Sew false corners at the bottom. Unfold and sew across, as explained in Tea-Towel Tote on pages 34–35. Do not cut away the corners because they help maintain the shape of the bag. If you want you can cut a piece of cardboard and cover it with fabric to reinforce the bottom of the bag.

Sew together the opening from the strap to the side seam by hand with invisible stitches through the sides and strap.

Mini Purses

I use these mini purses when I am travelling. They are very useful for keeping all the family's props in one place. They can be used to hold:
• First aid items, headache pills, wipes
• Passport, tickets, boarding cards
• Small toys that keep the kids busy for a long time: playing cards, cars, hand-held computer games, marbles, pencils
• Hair ties, lip gloss, hand cream, hair clips, eyeliner, nail files
• Suncream, sunblock, sunglasses
• Different foreign currencies in different purses
• Visa, health records, insurance card
• Mobile (cell) phone
• Camera, memory cards, batteries
• Asthma medication
• Pen, paper, local stamps
• Hotel keys, cash and credit cards
• CDs and DVDs
• Sewing things and needlework
• Clothes pegs and washing powder

Every time we are going somewhere new, regardless of whether it is on a plane, to the beach, to a bar, to the shops, a day trip or to the playground, I quickly pack together what we need with us and leave whatever we do not at home. It is so much easier to find what I am looking for when everything is organized.

Mini purse
You will need:
• Zip, 5½in (14cm)
• Two pieces of fabric with fusible interfacing ironed on, 6½ x 5¼in (18.5 x 13.5cm)

Pencil case
You will need:
• Zip, 8in (20cm)
• Two pieces of fabric with fusible interfacing ironed on, 10 x 4¼ (26.5 x 11.5cm)
• Two pieces of fabric with fusible interfacing ironed on, 1½in (4cm) x zip width

Instructions:
I used stiff fusible interfacing to make the fabric stronger, the same type that is inside cuffs and collars. When you have ironed on the interfacing you do not have to fold hems or sew zigzag overlocking. The fabric will not fray or tear if the interfacing is attached properly with an iron. This makes the mini purses very easy and fast to make compared to traditional quilting with wadding (batting) and linings. To use patchwork on the purse is unnecessary, as the fabric is the decoration in itself.

Make sure the colours of the fabric and the zip go together. It is always easiest to have the zip as a starting point and then find a fabric that matches. You find zips in a limited choice of colours, while there are hundreds of different fabrics. Choose a thread to sew the zip in the same colour as the zip. Use light threads for the rest of the seams, or the same colour as the fabric becomes on the reverse after the interfacing is ironed on.

Cut two separate pieces of fabric. Cut by hand approximately 2in (5cm) bigger than what it is supposed to be cut down to later. Cut the fusible interfacing so it is a little bit smaller than the fabric pieces. This is to avoid getting adhesive on the iron or the ironing board.

Press the interfacing to the wrong side of the fabric (this takes around eight minutes of pressing, not ironing).

Cut the fabrics so the width is the metal zip length plus the seam allowance at both ends. Cut the height to whatever measurement is desired. My measurements are a result of what zips I have to hand, how much interfacing I have in my drawer and what my fabric leftovers look like. Since they are leftovers they are in different shapes and sizes – you use what you have.

Begin with the zip closed. Place the zip and one of the fabric pieces right sides together and edge to edge and pin. Put a zipper foot on the sewing machine. Start sewing the zip from the end. Stop halfway with the needle down, lift up the foot and pull the zip loop away by opening it and place the loop where you have already sewn.

Sew the other piece of fabric to the zip. Make sure that the two pieces of fabric are placed directly opposite each other.

Place the purse pieces right sides together and sew the side seams. You can sew the side seams slightly inwards towards the top and zip so the purse will be closed on top. Open the zip so you can reverse your work at the end. Sew the bottom seam. Reverse and press.

You can also make end pieces on the zip. This makes the transition between the zip and the side seam look better at the top. The shape will change a little bit if you do this and the zip will not go all the way out. This is a way to make the purse bigger when the zip is not long enough.

A flat folder for travel documents and a little purse for needlework. It is important to have everything nearby when you feel like sewing. I have put everything I need for parts of different projects in cute little purses, so I can do some work whenever I have time. It is like an addiction – I get withdrawal symptoms if I don't have my needlework with me.

The end pieces are cut the same way as the other fabric pieces, with fusible interfacing. Put the piece right side to right side at the end of the zip and sew a seam right across. Fold out and press. Do the exact same thing on the other end. Continue as described earlier. Cut away the excess end pieces.

Another alternative is to cut the fabric in one piece, so that you do not have to sew the bottom seam. Cut a piece the same width but twice the height and also use end pieces on the zip. See the striped purse on page 54.

Green pencil case

You will need:
• Zip, 8½in (22cm). This is a plastic zip that was originally longer. I sewed over the end in the side seam and put it inside the case without cutting it off
• One piece of fabric with fusible interfacing ironed on, 9½ x 8¼in (24.5 x 22cm)

Sew the zip along the longest side.

Case for travel documents and passport (see page 55)

You will need:
• Zip, 9¼in (24cm)
• One piece of fabric with fusible interfacing ironed on, 12¾ x 12½in (33 x 32cm)
• Two pieces of fabric with fusible interfacing ironed on, 1¾in (5.5cm) x zip width

Sew the zip along the longest side.

Travel purse for needlework (see page 55)

You will need:
• Zip, 9in (23cm)
• Two pieces of fabric with fusible interfacing ironed on, 10 x 8¼in (26 x 22cm)

Sew the zip along the longest side.

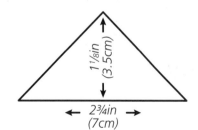

False bottom

Make a bottom in the purse by sewing a 90-degree seam at the bottom in each side seam. Illustrated you can see how I first traced the seam with a pencil. At the end the whole pencil case will be pressed. The interfacing makes it stay in shape.

Notice how the shape changes with the false bottom seam. The only thing that makes this purse different in shape to the one on page 52 is the false bottom. Putting in the false bottom requires you to allow a little more fabric in both height and width, as some fabric disappears inside the shape.

Coffee time

A small purse for sugar and little chocolates or biscuits.

You will need:
• Zip, 7½in (19.5cm)
• One piece of fabric with fusible interfacing ironed on, 9¾ x 10in (25.5 x 26.5cm)
• Two pieces of fabric with fusible interfacing ironed on, 1¼in (4cm) x zip width

Sew the zip along the shortest side.

Laundry day

This purse contains clothes pegs and packets of washing powder for when travelling with limited luggage space.

You will need:
• Zip, 6in (15.5cm)
• One piece of fabric with fusible interfacing ironed on, 7½ x 10¾in (19.5 x 28.5cm)
• Two pieces of fabric with fusible interfacing ironed on, 1¼in (4cm) x zip width

Sew the zip along the shortest side.

Tip
Use oilcloth fabric to make practical little beach bags for wet swimwear.

1¾in (4.5cm)
← 3½in →
(9cm)
False bottom for Coffee Time

'Home is Best' Cushion

This cushion in flannel is big and soft and sits in a chair in front of the fireplace. The text reads 'east, west, home is best' in Norwegian but you could easily change it to English if you prefer.

You will need:
• 48 different pieces of flannel, approximately 8 x 6in (20 x 15cm)
• Fusible web
• Four different strips, approximately 2¾ x 12in (7 x 30cm), for the ties
• Backing flannel, 24 x 27½in (60 x 70cm)
• Wadding (batting), 24 x 27½in (60 x 70cm)
• Extra fabric in flannel, 24 x 20in (60 x 50cm)
• Inner cushion, approximately 26 x 22in (66 x 55cm). These is not a standard size – I folded an old down duvet to the size I wanted. You can also shake the down into one corner and sew around until you get the size you want (see page 91). I chose to focus more on the design of the cushion instead of standard sizes

Instructions:
Cut 24 flannel rectangles, measuring 6 x 4½in (16 x 12cm). Sew them together into one piece – four rows with six pieces in each row.

If you want to appliqué the letters on the pieces before you sew it all together, think carefully about the letters that cross more than one piece. You will not be able to attach these before all the pieces are put together.

Cut a piece of wadding (batting) a little bit bigger than the front piece and tack it to the reverse side.

Trace the letters, the parts for the house and four hearts on the paper side of the fusible web. Cut out roughly. Iron each letter on the wrong side of its fabric piece. Cut out precisely following the pencil line. Remove the paper. Iron the letters in their right places. Notice that some of the letters cover parts of other pieces. The dot above the letter j is placed a little off-centre. Sew around all the letters and motifs with appliqué stitches. The sewing machine will easily sew through the wadding (batting). If you want to do the stitching by hand, you might want to tack the wadding to the reverse side afterwards. Different types of wadding require different approaches, so experiment with various types and the stitches needed.

Quilt all the seams. If you sew on the letters without the wadding (batting) behind, you should quilt around the letters as well.

Trim the front side and then cut the backing the same size. Cut two extra fabrics in different sizes: 'short side of front side' x 5in (13cm) and 'long side of front side' x 11in (28cm).

Cut the ties in four different fabrics, 2½ x 11in (6.5 x 28cm). Fold them lengthways right sides together and sew along one short end and the whole long side. Reverse and press.

Zigzag stitch all the parts except the ties. Fold in one of the long sides on each of the extra fabrics. Place the biggest extra fabric on the front piece right sides together and put two ties in the seam at the same time, see diagram on page 62. Reverse and press. Do the same thing with the backing and the smallest extra fabric. Make sure the ties end up in the same place.

Place the whole cushion's front side on a table with the right side facing up. The extra fabric is lying as an extension of the front piece with the right side forwards. Place the backing on top with the reverse side facing up. The extra

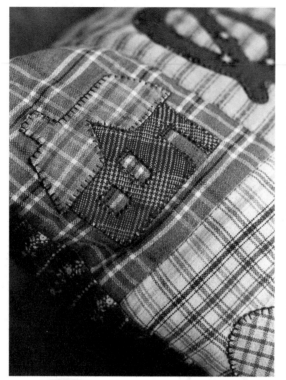

A cute house motif placed in the corner of the cushion. I used machine appliqué stitches.

Notice that some of the letters go over more than one piece of fabric. The extra fabric and the ties make a closing mechanism. If you think this method seems difficult, you can use an old shirt for the back, as described on page 38.

fabric that is sewn to the backing should fold downwards so you will see the extra fabrics' right side and the wrong side of the backing. Above this you can see the front piece's extra fabric with the right side up.

Take this extra fabric and fold it down over everything. You can now only see the wrong side of the backing and the wrong side of the front piece's extra fabric.

Pin and sew around three sides through all layers. Sew all sides except the cushion's right side where the ties are. Make sure you do not include the ties when sewing.

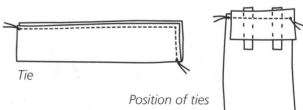

Tie

Position of ties and extra fabric

Reverse and press. Insert a cushion and tie the opening together with the ties.

The patterns are on pages 119–121.

Doll's Quilt

Size: approximately 12.5 x 15in (32 x 38.5cm) after washing and shrinkage.

This very easy geometrical pattern is a great way to show off four fabrics you think look harmonious and beautiful together when you don't have a huge amount of them. Easy quilting creates a lattice design.

You will need:
• Light fabric with a large pattern, 4in (10cm)
• Medium light striped fabric, 4in (10cm)
• Medium dark border fabric with small flower pattern, 6in (15cm)
• Dark border fabric, 6in (15cm)
• Backing fabric and cotton wadding (batting), approximately 16 x 20in (40 x 50cm)

Cutting list:
• Cut three strips of light large patterned fabric, 2½ x 13½in (7 x 35cm)
• Cut two strips of striped fabric, one horizontal and one vertical to the stripes, 2½ x 13½in (7 x 35cm)
• Cut the medium dark border, 2in (6cm)
• Cut the dark border, 2in (6cm)

Sew the strips together, alternating light and medium light. Iron the seam allowance against the darkest fabric. Attach the borders on the long sides first, then top and bottom. Mark the top for quilting with a 1in (2.5cm) lattice pattern. Put the backing, wadding (batting) and front on top of each other and tack them together. Quilt by hand or on the sewing machine.

Alphabet Cushion

Size: approximately 11 x 11in (27.5 x 27.5cm) after washing and shrinkage.

This is a brilliant way to learn the alphabet. I used the leftover blocks from the 'Boy's Stuff' Quilt on page 46, once again put together to create something new.

You will need:
• Yellow alphabet fabric (or something else if this is impossible to find), 4in (10cm)
• Thin blue denim for the border, 8in (20cm)
• Blue checked fabric for the filler, 4in (10cm)
• Some grey, light and black fabric remnants for the blocks
• Small inner cushion, 12 x 12in (30 x 30cm)
• An old shirt for the backing

Cutting list:
• Cut four light and four dark pieces of fabric for the blocks, 1⅝ x 1⅝in (5 x 5cm)
• Cut two filler squares, 2¾ x 2¾in (8 x 8cm)
• Cut the alphabet border, 2¼in (6.5cm)
• Cut the denim border, 2in (6cm)

Instructions:
Piece the blocks and blue checked filler squares and apply the borders. The front side is padded with wadding (batting) the normal way. Quilt all seams and quilt over the filler squares to make them look like they are pieced in the same way as the blocks. Quilt the denim border with three parallel lines with a quilting foot's distance between them. These lines create a lattice in the corners.

Roughly cut out the shirt front and place on the front of the cushion, right sides together. Sew around the whole outer edge. Unbutton and turn right side out.

The reverse of the cushion is an old shirt where the buttons function as the opening mechanism. The pocket has been retained and can be used as a secret compartment.

The Wheels on the Bus

Size: approximately 13 x 7½in (34 x 19cm)

This zip-up case was originally sewn to carry a child's asthma inhaler equipment, but it can also function as a pencil case.

The process is similar to the Shoulder Bag on pages 50–51. The difference is that this case does not have a strap and the bottom is made slightly differently. The corners are cut away before you sew the bottom. It is a good idea to read through the instructions for the Shoulder Bag before starting this project.

You will need:
• Zip, 12in (30cm)
• Wadding (batting), 12 x 32in (30 x 80cm)
• Striped fabric, 12in (30cm)
• Dotted fabric for the lining and loop, 12in (30cm)
• Fabric for the bus, 8 x 4in (20 x 10cm)
• Two buttons for the wheels
• A leftover piece of wadding for the loop, approximately 4 x 2in (10 x 5cm)

Cutting list:
• Cut two pieces of striped fabric, 15 x 11in (38 x 28cm)
• Cut two pieces of dotted fabric for the lining, 15 x 11in (38 x 28cm)
• Cut two pieces of wadding, a fraction smaller than the fabric and lining
• Cut one piece of dotted fabric for the loop, 3 x 3in (8.5 x 8.5cm)
• Cut wadding for the loop, 2 x 1¼in (5 x 3cm)

Instructions:
Cut out the bus and sew it on to the centre of one of the striped pieces with appliqué stitches.

Place the piece with the bus right side to right side on the lining. Apply and iron the wadding (batting). Pin the layers and sew a seam at the top. Reverse and press. Tack the layers together. Make the back in the same way. It is not necessary to do the appliqué here, but embroidering the owner's name on it would be a nice idea. Sew on the buttons as the wheels.

Finish the two pieces. I used a light thread in some of the light stripes in the fabric. The whole bottom area is closely quilted for extra strength. If you quilt by hand you have to remember that the piece needs to be cut to 14 x 10in (35 x 25cm) later, therefore you need to secure the threads within this area. If you use the sewing machine you need to sew close zigzag stitches around three of the edges to secure the thread after you cut it.

Cut the pieces to 14 x 10in (35 x 25cm). Cut away the two lower corners as well, 2½ x 2½in (6.5 x 6.5cm). See photograph opposite.

Sew the loop. Fold it twice with the right side inwards and then sew along one side and reverse. Apply wadding (batting) and quilt as desired. The loop should be folded twice and put inside the side seam later, therefore the end does not have to look pretty.

Place the zip right side to right side against the lining. Switch to the zipper foot and sew on the zip with one line of stitching running all the way along, a seam allowance distance from the edge. As well as attaching the zip, the stitching also gives a decorative edge around the zip, allowing the inside of the bag to show a little bit. Sew the zip to one side at a time. The

two separate parts have now become one piece with a zip in between. The zip area is the only thing that is finished at this stage.

Refer to the photographs on page 50 to see how the fabrics lie around the wadding (batting) and how to sew on the zip. The photos show a different case in progress, but show you how to sew on the zip nicely before you do any further work.

Fold the case so the two sides lie right side to right side. Open the zip enough to reverse it later. Sew the side seams. Place the loop inside the seam on the side the zip 'handle' is located when the zip is closed. Sew the bottom together parallel with the zip. Then fold the bottom corners, pin and sew together. Sew over the seams with a close zigzag stitch with a toning thread.

The pattern is on page 118.

Beautiful Borders

This project started out with me playing with the fabrics and ended up with three quilts. The last one is still in progress.

The thought behind this project was to have simple rectangles that would make the fabrics stand out. Both quilts are put together after a round of cutting. As a result of different borders they have become quite different. This shows how important the border is.

These fabrics are fairly powerful and happy. Many of them are historical fabrics, which mean they are reproduced with old patterns from museums and archives. Sometimes they change the colour and sometimes it is an exact copy of the original. My fabrics are from 1790–1940. I am interested in using fabrics from different eras. I think it is more important that the colours and patterns fit together.

• Amy Butler fabric in turquoise and olive for the outer border, 16in (40cm)
• Backing fabric and cotton wadding (batting), 28 x 32in (70 x 80cm)

Cutting list:
• Cut 12 rectangles, 5½ x 4in (15 x 11cm)
• Cut six rectangles, 5½ x 2½in (15 x 7cm)
• Cut two narrow borders, one yellow and one blue, 2½in (7cm)
• Cut one red checked and one green checked border, 3¾in (10.5cm)
• Cut two blue checked borders, 4½in (12cm)
• Cut the outer border, 2¼in (6.5cm)

The patchwork is done on a sewing machine with quilting in all seams and geometrical patterns within the rectangles. The borders are quilted with lengthways lines that follow the squares in the pattern. The thread colours are adjusted to each fabric.

Borders 1

Size: approximately 26 x 24in (66 x 60cm)

This cheerful quilt with several vibrant colours in the border can be used as a cot blanket or a tablecloth.

You will need:
• Eight different fabrics in pink, blue, green, flax and bright yellow for the rectangles, 8in (20cm)
• Yellow and blue fabric for the narrow borders, 4in (10cm)
• Red checked and green checked fabric for the borders, 6in (15cm)
• Blue checked fabric for the borders, 12in (30cm)

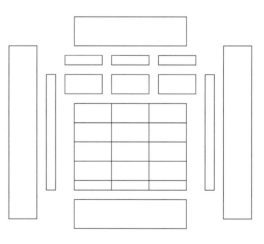

Piecing diagram

Borders 2

Size: approximately 32 x 22in (81 x 55cm)

This quilt with a striped border can be used as a cot blanket or a tablecloth.

You will need:
• Eight different fabrics in pink, blue, green, flax and bright yellow for the rectangles, 8in (20cm)
• Green fabric for the narrow border, 8in (20cm)
• Blue striped fabric for the border, 20in (50cm)
• Dotted fabric for the outer border, 16in (40cm)
• Backing fabric and cotton wadding (batting), 30 x 40in (75 x 100cm)

Cutting list:
• Cut 20 rectangles, 5½ x 4in (15 x 11cm)
• Cut the light green border, 1¾in (5.5cm)
• Cut the blue striped border, 3¾in (10cm)
• Cut the dotted border, 2¼in (6.5cm)

Machine quilt all seams and add decorative quilting in all the borders. Use an adhesive tear-away quilting pattern in the striped border. Notice that the pattern in this border does not fill enough of the width. I solved this by adding a 'filler' line towards the green side, so that the area is visually filled with quilting without me having to change my mind on the quilting pattern I wanted. Adhesive tear-away quilting patterns are available in several patterns and widths. I sometimes adjust the width of the border so a pattern fits perfectly, but usually I decide the border width based on how I think the fabric fits visually with the quilt's patterns and colours. Other times the width of the border is a result of how much fabric I have left.

Inspiration for Beautiful Borders

I collect pictures with beautiful colour combinations, for example from newspaper advertisements and from magazines. It can also be a good idea to save line drawings for inspiration. Also, pictures of old quilts are always a good source of inspiration.

The quilt pictured below was made by Turid Øverland when she was in primary school in Oslo, Norway in the mid 1970s. The quilt is impulsive and mischievous. Turid tells me her teacher let her go on until she had taken out all the orange, brown and green fabrics from the leftovers boxes. Her aunt also contributed a few patches. She never thought of buying new fabrics.

This quilt inspired me so much that Beautiful Borders came to life 30 years later. My quilts do not look like Turid's, but they tell the same story. They are influenced by our surroundings.

Hand-Sewn Coaster

With just an old piece of flax fabric and a few simple tacking stitches you can make a pretty sailing-themed coaster.

To transfer the pattern to the fabric, draw the boat motif onto a piece of paper. Tape the paper to a sunny window and tape the fabric on top. Trace the pattern lightly with a pencil.

Embroider with wool thread using tacking stitches. It does not matter if the knot shows on the top side.

The pattern is on page 116.

Quick Key Ring

Jazz up your keys with this quick project, using a beautiful ribbon, some pretty buttons and a plain key ring.

Sew some stitches down the edges of the ribbon using wool thread. Thread the key ring onto the ribbon, fold it double and tie in a knot. Adjust the length of the ribbon depending on its thickness. Make the knot before you make the final cut. The width of the ribbon requires different lengths to make a nice result. The ribbon in the photograph is first cut to 16in (40cm) and then adjusted down to 14in (36cm).

Secure the ends by sewing two buttons back to back. Hem the ends of the ribbon or just cut them diagonally. Fold the ribbon ends in between the buttons to finish.

You can also use a strip of wool felt for the key ring. Choose wool that is felted so that the ends will not fray.

Simple Pincushions

Size: approximately 5 x 5½in (13 x 13.5cm)

This project features basic appliqué work with tacking stitches mounted as a pincushion. An old shirt front with buttons was used for the backs. My niece Hilda-Marie, 5, and nephew Espen, 3, did the appliqué work by themselves, though Espen needed some help from his mum and his Aunt Titti (me!). The kids chose the fabrics and the thread colour. I sewed the edges on the reverse side against the shirt front and placed a cushion inside. We wrapped the pincushions and put them under the Christmas tree for mum and dad who were very proud of what their children had made. The pincushions are displayed on the bookshelf so that everybody can admire them!

It is easiest to use checked fabric for the cushion. This makes it easier for children to sew in a straight line. The appliqué stitches are sewn with wool thread and a big needle. Use fusible web for the appliqué work and add quilt wadding (batting) behind the front piece.

The pattern is on page 116.

Button Mittens

When I designed these mittens, I had in mind to embroider the cuffs, but with time being at a premium, buttons work as an excellent quick alternative. When you wear these mittens you will find that people start chatting with you – they are a real conversation starter!

Knit the mittens the usual way, but make the ribbed border in the following way: start with a few ribs and then knit stocking stitches. Bind each side so the ribbed border becomes like a fanned cuff. See diagram. Cut two pieces of wool felt a little smaller than the cuffs and appliqué them with rough stitches in wool thread. Sew on buttons until you have covered most of the surface. Fill any gaps with simple wool cross stitches and/or embroider your initials.

A special thank you to my grandma who did the knitting and to Irene who had the idea.

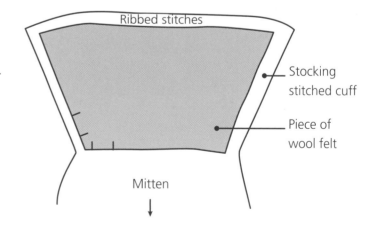

Ribbed stitches

Stocking stitched cuff

Piece of wool felt

Mitten

Button Bracelet

It is easier to get a pretty result if you use buttons with four holes, but you can also use buttons with two holes if you have to. Buttons with two holes turn around more easily, so the reverse side faces up.

Use a waxed thread and cut two separate lengths measuring 16in (40cm). When shopping for the thread, bear in mind that the thread you use must fit through the buttonholes. You can use sticky tape at the end of the string if it is too slack. Thread one of the strings diagonally through two holes in each button. Thread the other string diagonally through the other two holes. Tie the strings together at each end before you tie the ends together to make a circle. Make the bracelet just big enough to get it over the wearer's wrist. I used ten buttons in this bracelet. Use only one string if the buttons you use have two holes and not four. Tie it together in a circle with a reef knot.

Thanks to Line and Marie who gave me the idea.

Marbles Pouch

This pouch is lying under the bracelets in the photograph above.

You will need:
• Zip, 6in (15cm)
• Two pieces of fabric with fusible interfacing ironed on, 6½ x 4¼in (17 x 12cm)

See Mini Purses on pages 53–54 for instructions.

Pretty Pincushions

Use a spare block or sew an easy four-patch block to make these lovely hanging pincushions. Ribbons placed in the seam give you loops so you can hang them up. I have all my pincushions hanging on button pegs on the wall by my sewing machine, so that I always have somewhere to put pins while I am sewing.

Attach the ribbon loop to the front side so it will be included in the seam later. Place the back piece and front piece – with the loop – right side to right side and sew around. Remember to leave a small opening to turn it right side out later. Secure the threads well at the beginning and end of the stitching line. Sew false bottoms in all corners – see Mini Purses for instructions (page 56). Turn right side out. Tuck the seam allowance into the reversing opening and iron. This makes it easier to sew it together nicely later.

Cut an old wool sock into tiny pieces and use this as stuffing. Stitch up the reversing opening by hand.

You will need:

Beige squares (1)
• Two light and two dark squares, 2 x 2in (6 x 6cm)
• Ribbon loop, 4in (11cm)
• Back piece, same size as finished block
False bottom corner seam, ¾in (2cm)

Red triangle (2)
• Red crooked square, 2¾in (8cm)
• Ribbon loop, 3in (8.5cm)
• Back piece, same size as finished block
False bottom corner seam, ¾in (2cm)

This pincushion is special. It is sewn from a small piece of a handmade quilt. Thank you Cecilie.

Olive and blue four patch (3)
• Two olive and two light blue squares, 1½ x 1½in (4.5 x 4.5cm)
• Two beige squares, 3 x 3in (8 x 8cm). Cut the squares diagonally and sew in pairs on opposite sides. Trim the block to 3½in (9.5cm) so you get seam allowance in the corners
• Ribbon loop, 3½in (9.5cm)
• Back piece, same size as finished block
False bottom corner seam, 1in (2.5cm)

Red and white hand quilted (4)
• Red fabric, 3 x 2¾in (8 x 7.5cm)
• White fabric, 1½ x 2¾ (4.5 x 7.5cm)
• Ribbon loop, 3½in (9.5cm)
• Back piece, same size as finished block
False bottom corner seam, ½in (1.5cm)

Large pincushion (5)
• One block from 'Boy's Stuff' Quilt, page 46
• Ribbon loop, 4in (11cm)
• Back piece, same size as finished block
False bottom corner seam, 1¾in (4.5cm)

Squares and flowers (6)
• Two blue and two light squares, 2 x 2in
(6 x 6cm)
• Ribbon loop, 3½in (9.5cm)
• Back piece, same size as finished block
False bottom corner seam, ¾in (2cm)

Plagiarism
Writing a book is a long process. First I sew
the models, then they are photographed and
then I write the text before it is printed. While
I was writing this book I almost choked on my
coffee when I saw a picture of my pincushions
in the June 2006 issue of *American Patchwork
& Quilting Magazine*. At least they looked
very similar. The woman that had made the
pincushions has of course not copied me nor
have I copied her. It is just by coincidence that
we had the same idea.

*I cut up old knitted sweaters into small pieces
and use it as filling in pincushions. The pins
slide easily into this material.*

Needlework Jars

At flea markets or in basements, you can
often find beautiful old jars. I removed the
rubber washer and glass lid and replaced them
with two pieces of cardboard for each jar.
The cardboard is cut using the glass lid as a
template. One is a bit smaller than the other.

Sew a block in log cabin technique using the
pattern on page 82. Cutting measurements are
1in (3cm). I used the sew-on-paper technique.

You can also sew the block by hand. Each strip
measures ⅜in (1cm) when it is finished. In
addition to the centre piece I used three rounds
of light fabric and three rounds of dark. All the
fabrics are different. The block is placed on a
larger piece of cotton wadding (batting) and
quilted in the seams. Leave the wadding outside
of the block. Cut several layers of wadding and
put it behind the quilted block until you reach
the desired height. The pins are only supposed

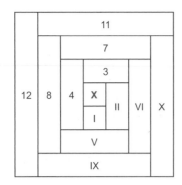

		11			
12	8	7			
		3			
		4	X	II	VI	X
			I			
		V			
		IX			

*Log cabin block piecing
diagram (see also page 107)*

and put it behind the quilted block until you reach the desired height. The pins are only supposed to be in the wadding, not in the card. Cut the pieces of wadding for the height into nice circles using the small piece of cardboard as a template.

Place the circles of wadding (batting) underneath the block and place the smallest piece of cardboard behind the wadding. Attach the wadding with tacking stitches in all directions on the reverse, see diagram below. When you have centred the block and made it look nice within the metal circle you can decorate the inside of the lid. Use the biggest piece of cardboard. I pressed the cardboard in place inside the lid, just enough for it to lie in the space between the grooves and the block, wadding and the metal circle. Alternatively you can use a glue gun.

Fill the jar with reels of thread and put pins on top. This is a great gift for anyone that is interested in needlework. The jars are very decorative so you can have them out and accessible at all times.

Thanks to Uncle Gunnar, Aunt Lillian and Siri for the jars.

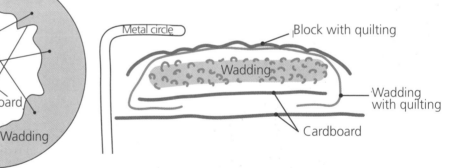

Pig Frame

I had a few blocks leftover from my Miniature Log Cabin Blocks projects (see pages 105–107). One of them has been used in this pig frame. The aperture is rectangular but the block is square, so I sewed a strip on each side of the block. The mounting is the same as on the jars (see above) except the wadding (batting). The wadding is unnecessary because the cardboard, adhesive, tape and tacking keep it in place. I removed the glass and used it as a template to cut out the cardboard. Make sure that the block plus the cardboard will fit inside the frame.

Leftovers Cushion

Size: approximately 15½ x 15½in (39 x 39cm)

One side is a leftover 9 x 9in (23 x 23cm) churn dash block mounted on point and the other side is an old shirt.

You will need:
• Striped light blue flannel for the block, 6in (15cm)
• Dark green checked flannel for the block, 6in (15) cm
• Medium tone khaki for the block, 4in (10cm)
• Brown fabric with a small-scale flower pattern for the on-point mounting, 10in (25cm)
• Striped fabric for the outer border, 4in (10cm)
• Cotton wadding (batting), 20 x 20in (50 x 50cm)
• Shirt front for the backing, 20 x 20in (50 x 50cm)
• Inner cushion, 16 x 16in (40 x 40cm)

Cutting list:
• Cut one square in striped light blue flannel, 3½ x 3½in (9.5 x 9.5cm)
• Cut two squares in light blue flannel, 4 x 4in (12 x 12cm)
• Cut two squares in dark green checked flannel, 4 x 4in (12 x 12cm)
• Cut four rectangles in light blue flannel, 2 x 3½in (5.75 x 9.5cm)
• Cut four rectangles in medium tone khaki, 2 x 3½in (5.75 x 9.5cm)
• Cut two squares in brown flowery fabric, 8 x 8in (20 x 20cm)
• Cut the striped outer border, 1½in (4.5cm)

Intructions:
Make four half square triangle units of two light and two dark squares: Place one dark and one light square (4 x 4in/10 x 10cm) on top of each other right sides together. Draw a diagonal with a pencil and ruler, making sure the line goes from point to point, see page 124.

Sew a seam allowance distance from the line on both sides. Cut along the line. Open the triangle and press. Trim the half square triangle units to 3½ x 3½in (9 x 9cm).

Sew together one light and one medium light rectangle into a double side edge. Make four.

Follow the diagram on page 124 and sew the block together. Make sure the half square triangle units face the right way.

Cut the two brown flowery squares in half diagonally. Sew the four triangles on opposite sides so the block is mounted on point. Trim the entire front piece so that the finished size will fit the cushion after the outer border is sewn on. Notice that my block is floating in the brown fabric and that the points do not go all the way out to the edge. Sew on the outer border.

The front side has a layer of cotton wadding (batting) on the reverse side and is quilted in all seams. It is also quilted a seam allowance distance in some places. The brown fabric is quilted with a simple striped pattern which goes in different directions in each of the different triangles.

See page 38 for instructions on how to mount a shirt front.

Cute Sweater

A normal wool sweater is decorated with an appliqué. I also decorated it with some tacking stitches in wool thread around the wrists.

I did not use fusible web on this sweater. I cut the fabric for the face and ears using a cardboard template and attached the pieces with pins. I sewed the stitches on the face using water-soluble stabilizer (which disappears after washing). Use wool thread for the hair and facial features.

After making this sweater, I found out that spray adhesive and water-soluble stabilizer can leave sticky marks on woolen fabrics after washing. You should try out all aids with the materials you are planning to use. I failed to do that in this case. After washing it a few times it is almost gone, but I promise you it taught me a lesson! If in doubt trace the design with a pencil onto waxed paper.

The pattern is on page 116.

Button Art

I collect things I can use to display fabrics. It can be photo frames, cross stitch frames or any type of hangers. Flea markets, needlework stores and gift shops are all good places to look.

On a small island in Norway called Vesterøy there is a little gift shop. I found this handmade frame there one summer and now use it to display a few selected buttons.

Remove the glass and back plate. Cut a piece of fabric big enough to fit around the back plate and be tightened with tacking stitches. Do not attach anything yet. Draw a line with a pencil right outside the frame aperture so you know where the frame will sit when you attach the buttons. But make sure to place the pencil line so it is hidden behind the frame.

Choose fabric and buttons that reflect the colour and shape of the frame. My buttons are placed following the striped fabric and in a three by three pattern. I am sure a random placement of the buttons could work just as well. Place thin cotton wadding (batting) behind

the fabric and sew on the buttons with contrasting thread and visible knots and thread ends. Place the fabric with the buttons right side down. Place the back plate on top, making sure it is central, fold the fabric in around the edges and attach with tacking stitches. Turn over and mount in the frame.

Denim Patch

Size: approximately 15 x 15in (38 x 38cm) after washing and shrinkage.

You will need:
• Denim fabric, 12in (30cm)
• Four different green fabrics in checked, striped and flowered patterns, 6in (15cm) of each
• Blue patterned fabric for the border, 6in (15cm)
• Backing fabric and thin wadding (batting), 20 x 20in (50 x 50cm)

Cutting list:
• Cut the centre piece from denim, 9½ x 9½in (25 x 25cm)
• Cut four edge pieces from the different green fabrics, 3½ x 12½in (10 x 32cm)

Instructions:
Sew the first edge on the right side of the centre piece so the superfluous fabric peeks out at the top. Sew this piece to the last edge at the very end. Leave a seam allowance at the top of the first strip. You need this space to sew onto later (see diagrams).

I machine quilted a check pattern at the edges of the quilt. The denim was quilted using a template. The pattern was transferred with tailor's chalk. The easiest way is to find a template you like and then adjust the quilt's measurements to fit. Or you could use my drawing and transfer it to denim by using water-soluble stabilizer, wax paper, tulle or a light table.

The pattern is on page 118.

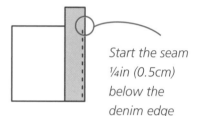

Start the seam ¼in (0.5cm) below the denim edge

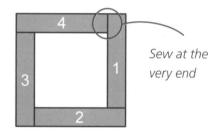

Sew at the very end

Boy's Pyjamas

Like the blazer on 39, these pyjamas had an emblem I did not like. This truck was made to cover it up. Unfortunately, I used leather buttons as wheels. They cannot be washed as they will leave ugly light brown stains. It is on my agenda to change them, I just haven't got round to it yet.

These pyjamas open at the front which makes it possible to put them flat into the sewing machine. This makes it easier to appliqué the chest area. By contrast, the blazer on page 39 could not fit in the sewing machine so I sewed that by hand.

Draw the truck on the paper side of some fusible web, cut it out roughly, iron against the truck fabric's reverse side, trim and remove the paper and iron on to the pyjamas.

On the pattern, the dotted line indicates an overlap. Cut out the pieces separately and put over each other. You will notice that there is a small space between the cabin and the truck. You will not find this in the pattern. I always draw a paper pattern before I make the fabric pieces.

I sometimes change my mind while I work, as I did here. I let the drawing differ from the project on purpose to tell you something about this. Even if you have already decided on an appliqué design, I think you should always move the pieces around before you iron. Sometimes you can find better solutions. Try this out, for example, with a flower appliqué. Perhaps one petal should point in another direction when you see what fabric it is cut from and the fabric it is lying on or against.

Place tear-away stabilizer on the wrong side of the pyjamas, this makes it easier. Experiment with different stitches and stitch widths/lengths until you find one that fits. Use the embroidery needle on the sewing machine and a slightly thicker silk or wool thread. Learn the rhythm of the stitch so you will be able to make nice turns. You always need to know where the needle is going. Get comfortable with the stitch before you start sewing on the pyjamas. Use the same type and colour of thread over and under. That way trouble with the thread tension or the settings will not show as much on the surface. Using the same quality for the thread over and under will make it easier to balance the stitches. If you are sewing appliqué stitches it is a good idea to loosen the thread tension, or tighten the thread tension underneath. This way knots and uneven loops will be pulled down and not seen on the surface.

The pattern is on page 116.

Angel Cushion

Size: approximately 20 x 14in (50 x 35cm).

You will need:
• Various strips in light colours for the centre panel, finished size 9½ x 15in (25 x 39cm)
• Dark fabric for the inner border, 6in (15cm)
• Checked fabric for the outer border, 6in (15cm)
• Four different pieces of red fabric for the corners, 2 x 2in (5 x 5cm)
• Fabric for the angel's skin, 4in (10cm)
• Fabric for the angel's dress, 6in (15cm)
• Fabric for the angel's wings, 4in (10cm)
• Backing fabric, approximately 26 x 20in (65 x 50cm) (or an old shirt front)
• Wadding (batting) for behind the front piece, approximately 26 x 20in (65 x 50cm)
• A little wool as angel hair
• Inner cushion

Instructions:
The centre panel is sewn together from leftover strips in widths of 1¼in (3.5cm), 1½in (4.5cm) and 1¾in (5.5cm). The centre panel needs to measure 9½ x 15in (25 x 39cm) after the strips are sewn together. Get as close to this measurement for the centre panel as possible with your own strips. Alternatively you can use a whole piece of fabric that is not patched.

The inner border is cut 2¼in (6.5cm) wide. The outer border is cut 1½in (4.5cm) wide. Cut the red corners 1½ x 1½in (4.5 x 4.5cm). Sew the corners on each side of the outer border's short sides. Sew the long sides of the border first, then the short sides with red corners.

The angel is added using normal appliqué techniques. Make several face samples, draw

This angel cushion was made by Tullemor Møller and is pictured here with her permission.

on them and pick the one you like best. Include some wool hair when you iron the face. See a close-up of the cushion on page 2.

I tacked cotton wadding (batting) under the whole front piece and appliquéd with the sewing machine through the front piece and wadding. The cushion is quilted in all seams. I did not quilt across the angel, even though there are seams underneath her. Against the dark border I chose to sew a round of appliqué stitches as a combination of quilting and decorative feature.

You can mount the cushion with backing fabric, or using a shirt front, as described on page 38.

If the inner cushion does not have standard measurements you can solve that in one of two ways. You can buy a down cushion that

is too big. Working from one corner, mark the required measurements onto the cushion with tailor's chalk. Shake the cushion so the down falls into this corner and keep the down in place with large pins. Do the same process in the opposite corner to keep the excess down away. Sew two parallel seams following your marks. Cut in the middle of the seams. Sew a outer zigzag seam. Hopefully will the rest of the cushion will come to use in another project!

The other option is to do as I usually do: buy a cushion that almost fits. Fold and push it around a little bit. Fill the bottom of the cushion cover with some strips of wadding (batting). I rolled up wadding in 16in (40cm) widths and stuffed these in to the edges where the cushion was a little lean.

The pattern is on page 126.

Appliqué Tea Towels

This project was designed for my sewing circle. We never really do much sewing, we just chat, reminisce and go on trips together. But sometimes the other women want me to arrange Christmas decoration workshops. I have to keep the projects simple. One Christmas we did appliqué on tea towels.

Wash and iron the towels before you appliqué on them. Choose a motive that fits, considering the lines and squares that are already woven into the towel. Also choose fabrics and threads that reflect the colour of the towel.

Draw hearts/angels on the paper side of the fusible web, cut out roughly and iron against the heart/angel fabrics reverse sides. Trim, remove the paper and iron onto the towel. The pieces are cut out separately and put over each other.

Appliqué by hand with two strands of wool thread, rough tacking stitches and visible knots.

Light blue haloes were embroidered with tacking stitches above the angels' heads. The facial features were drawn with textile pen.

The women from the same circle did some voluntary work sewing borders before the photo shoot for this book. Thanks to Anita, Elisabeth, Hilde and Jorunn.

The pattern is on page 125.

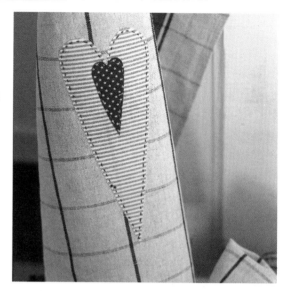

Heart motifs are easy to cut out and appliqué onto tea towels or any object – see the throw on page 41 and the pincushions on page 75.

The loop on this towel was not very nice. We solved that by sewing a ribbon over the existing loop. Ugly loops and washing instructions do not look good on hand-sewn towels.

Pair of Potholders

Size: approximately 9 x 9in (23 x 23cm).

It seems to be an unwritten rule that potholders always have to come in pairs. These two have two different sides, which all match my kitchen, different seasons and each other. Notice that the border is different on each one. I spent far more time deciding the colours for these potholders than I did actually sewing them. But that does not matter, picking colours is fun!

The wadding (batting) chosen for the potholders should fit their purpose. Are you planning to use them or are they for decoration only? Synthetic wadding is often completely useless, as synthetic material actually transmits heat meaning you will burn your fingers. However, there are some types of synthetic wadding that are designed for insulation you can try. Thick layers of wool or cotton are best for potholders. My preference is for a thick, firm cotton wadding.

You will need:
• Four different fabrics for four different sides, 12in (30cm)
• Some fabric leftovers to do an appliqué design, if you want
• One small pack of cotton wadding (batting)
• Two different border fabrics, 8in (20cm)
• Fabric for the loops, 6in (15cm)

Potholder 1, side A

(This side is not shown in the picture.) Appliqué an angel or heart onto a piece of fabric measuring 9 x 9in (23 x 23cm). Use any of the angel or a heart patterns in this book and adjust the size on a photocopier.

Potholder 1, side B

One piece of fabric (the same as the one used in the four-patch block on potholder 2).

Potholder 2, side A

A simple four-patch block. Pieces measuring 4¾ x 4¾in (13.5 x 13.5cm)

Potholder 2, side B

(This side is not shown in the picture.) One piece of fabric.

As you will need to quilt through the wadding (batting) and both sides at once, it is best that one side of each potholder is made from only one fabric. Think about what threads you want to use at the same time as you are picking the fabrics. The effect of the border and loop should be to lift the design. Construct the loop (see diagrams below) and attach in the seam on the border. Finish by sewing the border by hand on side B of each potholder. Cutting measurements for the loop: two pieces each 7 x 1½in (18 x 4.5cm).

How to construct the loop

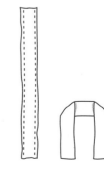

'Many Hands' Memory Quilt

A favourite teacher is leaving, a good colleague is moving on, an uncle turns 50, a confirmation or a wedding are all occasions that can be celebrated with a joint-effort quilt. As long as you can all manage to do some patchwork and are willing to make an effort, not much is required from each participator. You have to finish the quilt by sewing together all the appliqués and adding the border and backing. Beforehand you plan and prepare the appliqués.

Here is the story behind this pink 40th birthday quilt: The party was supposed to be a surprise dinner for Hilde with the girls from work, family and friends at a restaurant. Every guest was supposed to either give a speech or entertain with something during the dinner. This was made very clear in the invitation. Since I sew quilts, it was obvious to me that my contribution should be a quilt.

My plan was that everybody would appliqué a heart and then they could write a little greeting to the birthday girl inside the heart. I assumed that not everybody would be able to sew appliqué stitches, so I gave them other easier alternatives as well. I described in detail how to sew appliqué stitches (see page 99).

At home I prepared:
• As many textile markers as possible (borrowed from friends).
• Ready-made blocks with the hearts ironed on with fusible web. I made a few extra in case someone messed up their patch or wanted to change it.

• I prepared the blocks with ready-threaded needles and with embroidery thread in a suitable length.
• Pairs of scissors.
• Sheets of paper with writing and sewing instructions. Feel free to copy page 99 from this book and hand it out to the guests if you decide to do something similar.
• Pieces of fabric the guests could practice on before they write on the actual heart.

Think about the receiver's favourite colour. (Hilde's is pink and has always been pink).

Shape of the appliqué

Hearts are a good choice whenever there are girls and women involved. Boys and men can get car appliqués, or just a single square. Then the guests can just write directly on the patch. Make sure no one writes in the seam allowance.

Every rectangle is 7½ x 4½in (20 x 12cm). There were 16 guests plus me, so I used a four by four layout. I attached my heart to the backing as a signature.

If it is difficult to make the number of hearts add up you can add some neutral blocks between the heart blocks. You get uneven or even numbers by switching whether you start with a heart or not. It looks best if each corner either has a heart or not. Try out the layout on a table before you start sewing.

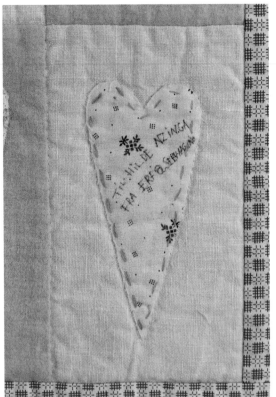

Everyone wrote a greeting to the birthday girl on their heart.

The appliqués were made by guests with different levels experience.

If there are any blocks leftover, make an additional gift such as a cushion or a cover for a photo album containing pictures from the party.

You can also attach any excess blocks to the backing. If planning to do this, make sure you check with the guests that they are happy for their work to go on the back.

Two vertical frames, 28½ x 3⅓in (67 x 10.5cm)
Two horizontal frames, 23 x 3¾in (59 x 10.5cm)

Anne-Kjersti Johansen gave me this idea when she made a memory quilt from a birthday celebrated in Italy. Thank you for the inspiration.

The pattern is on page 126.

Detail from the table runner on page 100, made using the leftover heart appliqués.

Heart Appliqué Instructions for Beginners

First task:

Write a greeting on the heart with a textile felt-tip pen. It is fine just to sign it, or you can include a little message if you want. Have a test-run on some scrap fabric first. It is easier to write if you move the pen downwards when you are writing. The texture of the fabric prevents you from doing your usual 'on paper' signature. You do not have to write in block letters, but it is harder not to.

Next task:

Appliqué the heart to the background. This can be done in several ways. I recommend using one of the following four methods:

A. Sew cross stitches along the outer edge of the heart.

B. Sew tacking stitches a short distance in from the edge.

C. Sew saddle stitches along the outer edge of the heart.

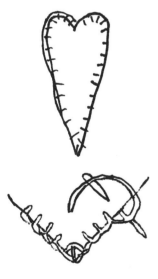

D. Sew appliqué stitches around the outer edge (this is where we see who was paying attention in home economics lessons at school!).

How to begin the appliqué stitch:

1. *Make a knot on the thread. Poke the needle through upwards by the edge of the heart from the wrong side.*
2. *Then push it down from above onto the heart at a 90-degree angle from the edge, (⅛–¼in) 3–4mm in.*
3. *Bring it upwards again almost where you first began – a little bit into the heart and to the left so the first 'stalk' is perpendicular.*

Now start the line of appliqué stitches:

4. *Poke the needle downwards into the heart, ¼in (0.5cm) from where you last did it.*
5. *Bring it up though the surface again at the edge of the heart. Pull while the loop at the edge is below the needle. One stitch complete! Continue doing the same around the whole heart.*

Hearts Table Runner

Size: approximately 20 x 61in (51 x 154cm) after washing and shrinkage.

While I planned and cut the memory quilt on page 96 for my friend's birthday, I made a few extra hearts just in case. I always do that when working on a project. To have some fun I decided to cut a few more backgrounds and introduce some new colours. What started out with pink and beige ended up with brown-grey, blue and a little orange. Ten of the hearts are used as end pieces for this table runner, and I will use the remaining four in another quilt.

I have made a few table runners with end pieces like this. By this, I am referring to the quilt's structure. In the large central piece there is really nothing going on except an interesting striped or checked fabric. The fun is in the end pieces. This structure makes it easier to have a vase of flowers or candles on the table. It can easily be too much if the table runner, vase and flowers are all competing for attention.

A good approach is to see if you have a checked patterned fabric that is wide enough for your table. If not, you have to buy fabric on the length of the roll. If you do this you will probably have enough to make several table runners. Measure the width that will fit for your table. Do not cut it exactly to size – leave some extra. Put the central piece aside and make the heart parts. Sew together and then cut the exact size for the central piece.

I have to admit I often do it the other way around. I have some leftovers I make into two end pieces and then find a central piece. The final length depends on whatever I can find in my fabric collection. And my collection is big…

You will need:
- Large checked fabric for central piece, approximately 24 x 52in (60 x 130cm)
- Four different heart backgrounds of pink linen, blue denim, flowered and checked light brown-grey, 8in (20cm) of each
- Fabric for the hearts (checked pink, striped and small-flowered, beige small-patterned, checked, light with red, light with peach and checked grey), 4in (10cm) of each
- Border fabric, 16in (40cm)
- Backing fabric and thin cotton wadding (batting), 26 x 67in (65 x 170cm)

Instructions:
Cut ten rectangles 4½ x 7½in (12 x 20cm). Draw ten hearts on fusible web. Cut out roughly. Iron to the heart fabrics' reverse side. Trim. Remove the paper and iron a heart to every background.

Make a few extra patches so you can try out different threads and stitches, particularly if you use a sewing machine. For this patch I used a felt stitch (in the appliqué settings) set to 5 in width, 1.5 in length and 1.2 in thread tension. I chose a thread that is similar to the background rectangle to create an illusion of hand stitches.

For the central piece, choose a checked fabric that reflects the colours used. Cut it as wide as five hearts sewn together x 50in (125cm) long.

Quilt in all seams, around the hearts and along the check lines in the central piece.

I chose the border carefully. It brings light and pink colour from the end pieces around the grey and lifeless central piece. It is cut 2¼in (6cm).

The pattern is on page 126.

Easter Table Topper

Size: 12 x 13in (30 x 33cm).

You will need:
- Linen, 12in (30cm)
- Olive flannel, 4in (10cm)
- Striped fabric, 4in (10cm)
- Yellow fabric, 4in (10cm)
- Checked grey-olive fabric for the border, 6in (15cm)
- Backing fabric and wadding (batting), approximately 16 x 16in (40 x 40cm)

Cutting list:
- Cut one piece of linen, 8¼ x 9in (22 x 24cm)
- Cut eight corner pieces in olive fabric and eight in striped fabric, 1½ x 1½in (4.5 x 4.5cm)
- Cut the yellow fabric 2½in (6.5cm) wide. Cut after you have sewn the corners, then measure the length

The centre piece is machine quilted with a template, which is transferred to the linen with a pencil. It is easiest to find a nice template and then adjust the topper's measurements accordingly. Or you can use my drawing and transfer it to your linen. Quilt all seams. I also quilted a line down the centre of the yellow fabric through the corner blocks.

The pattern is on page 123.

'Inspired by Anne' Pram Quilt

Size: approximately 26 x 26in (64 x 64cm) after washing and shrinkage.

I am exposed to lots of inspiration every day. Customers in my shop, seminar participants and colleagues show me their half-finished work and ask me for advice. Often this gives me inspiration to make something in similar colours or fabrics. Sometimes I sketch it down straight away. Other times I cannot tell where I got the idea from. I also occasionally have the same idea as someone else at the exact same time, where we both may claim to have had the idea first. Maybe it is inspiration from another place we did not know exists.

In this case the origin is known as I wrote it down in my sketch papers with cutting measurements. This little quilt came to this world because my colleague Anne-Kjersti had sewn a pram quilt, which she partly did because I introduced the expression 'free quilt' a few years ago, which in turn had inspired her.

This quilt fits a pram (baby carriage) perfectly and is suitable for winter and summer. Notice that the dark four-patch blocks are leftovers from the 'Boy's Stuff' Quilt on page 46.

You will need:
• Light fabric for the border, 12in (30cm)
• Beige fabric for the border, 12in (30cm)
• Red fabric for the corners, 6in (15cm)
• Blue fabric for the border, 12in (30cm)
• Striped red fabric for fillers, 6in (15cm)
• Olive green fabric, 12in (30cm)
• Blue, black and grey leftover fabrics for the four-patch blocks
• Backing fabric and thin cotton wadding (batting), 30 x 30in (75 x 75cm)

Cutting list:
• Cut 48 squares from the leftover fabrics for four-patch blocks, 1⅝ x 1⅝in (5 x 5cm).
• Cut 24 olive squares, 2¾ x 2¾in (8 x 8cm).
• Cut 13 squares from the striped red fabric, 3¾ x 3¾in (10 x 10cm).
• Cut the light border 2¼in (6.5cm) wide.
• Cut the beige border 3¾in (10.5cm) wide.
• Cut four red corner squares, 3¾ x 3¾in (10.5 x 10.5cm).

Instructions:
Begin with the four-patch blocks. Sew together the 48 squares to make 12 blocks and iron. Cut the olive squares in half diagonally. Sew the triangles to the sides of the four-patch blocks to mount them on point.

Trim the blocks to 3¾ x 3¾in (10 x 10cm). Make sure you centre the four-patch blocks and that you have enough seam allowance by each corner. Use other cutting measurements if that fits better with your seam allowance. Sew together the red squares and the sewn blocks in five rows of five pieces, alternating the position of the blocks and putting a red square in each corner (see diagram below). Both the stripes on the fabric and corners on the four-patch blocks should be sewn straight and precise. I aim towards following the fabrics' weave and the seams' crossovers.

Notice that sometimes the stripes in the red squares are vertical and sometimes they are horizontal. Also notice that the four-patch blocks' dark/light fabric does not face the same way everywhere. This is 'by coincidence' and gives the quilt a natural, free feel.

Every seam is machine quilted. The striped red squares and the beige border have got stitches along the weave in an even striped pattern. The red corner squares are quilted with a flower motif. Stitches also go along the light border.

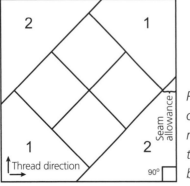

Piecing the on-point mounting for the four-patch block

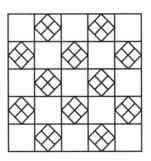

Blocks/fillers layout diagram

Miniature Log Cabin Blocks

Size of finished block: 3in (8cm).

These blocks are sewn on top of a layer of paper. I used squared paper, a photocopier and normal paper to multiply it. I found the fabrics in one of my leftovers boxes. The strips are 1in (3cm) wide and become ¾in (2cm) after they are finished. Around the central square I have three light rounds and three dark. Almost all the fabrics are different.

Sewing on paper means to place the fabric on the paper's reverse side and sew following the line on the paper's front side. Use stitch length 1.5 to perforate the paper, which is then removed after the blocks are sewn together. To be able to see the line through the paper you need to hold it against a light. There also exists a special paper for quilters that is transparent and easy to remove.

Following the diagram below, begin with the red fabric with the right side up at X.

Then, place a light fabric with the wrong side up in I. Sew the line between X and I. Let the stitch start a few millimeters before the line and run a few millimeters longer than the line. It is not necessary to secure the thread. Remove the work from the machine, press the strip with your fingers and trim the seam allowance. Press with an iron. From now on you place all the strips wrong side up. Continue with II, also in light fabric. The next one is 3 in dark fabric. Then another dark at 4, then a light one at V.

This is the logic: X is red and the centre of the block. Roman numerals are light fabrics. Normal figures are dark fabrics. The numbers show the stitching sequence.

Machine quilting

I have used two different thread colours and a normal thin cotton thread. I quilted in the ditch where there is no seam allowance (see page 17). Instead of crossing over whole patches I secured the thread and started again. The thread colour is light (golden beige) and dark (olive/charcoal). These two colours disappear in the fabrics. I padded all the blocks at the same time. I sewed all the light stitching first, then the dark. On the diagram below, light thread is marked with a red dotted line and dark thread is marked with a blue dotted line. When several blocks were sewn together I quilted the outer edge of the blocks too.

Tiny Table Runner (see page 105)

Size: approximately 6½ x 17in (16 x 43cm) after washing and shrinkage.

Five miniature log cabin blocks are sewn together in a strip. Darks and lights are turned around so a diagonal stripe effect appears. The blue border is cut 2in (6cm) wide. The blocks are quilted as described above. The border is quilted with an adhesive tear-away pattern. A striped white fabric is used for the border.

Rose Table Topper (opposite)

Size: approximately 15 x 15in (38 x 38cm) after washing and shrinkage.

I used my favourite rose pattern fabric around nine miniature log cabin blocks in a three-by-three block panel. The diagonal stripe effect is chosen for this table topper too. The border is cut 3¾in (10 cm) and quilted with an adhesive tear-away pattern (see page 18).

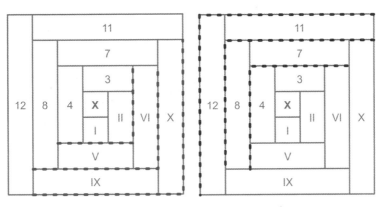

Miniature log cabin block – piecing and quilting diagram

Internet Stars Quilt

Size: approximately 54 x 87in (137 x 221cm) after washing and shrinkage.

In 2003, I participated in the start up of Quilt Scandinavia – an online exchange of blocks. We were supposed to sew star blocks and use repro fabrics in red, white and blue. The block should measure 9 x 9in (23 x 23cm) after it is sewn into a quilt, so a block ready for exchange had to measure 9½ x 9½ (25 x 25cm). Anne Mette was in charge of the practical arrangements, if I remember correctly. You would get just as many blocks in return as you had sent in. I was left with about 40 blocks, some of them I had sewn myself and some I got in my mailbox in return for what I had sent in. So far I have used them in two different quilts, but I still have several blocks left. You can see one of the quilts here.

You can arrange this type of block exchange in your sewing circle, handicraft group or similar. I made 13 of the blocks in this quilt, the other 10 I got from other people. This way the quilt gets a completely different impression than if I made all the blocks myself. Yet I feel the quilt is mine, I chose the blocks and put it together. It was a fun way to get some variation in my work.

I do not know who made which blocks, but these ladies are the contributors to the two quilts and leftover patches: Kimberly Pratt (USA), Kari Veslum (Norway), Helene Juul (Denmark), Jenny de Schutter (Belgium) and Marian Martzall (country unknown).

Quilt characteristics
The quilt consists of nine rows with five blocks on each row and alternates between star blocks and brown flower-pattern fabric. There is a total of 23 star blocks and 22 squares in brown fabric. A star block is placed in each corner. The cutting measurements for the brown fabric are 9½ x 9½in (25 x 25cm). The light border is 4¾in (13cm) wide. The outer border is pieced at the top and bottom with other fabrics, as I didn't have enough of the checked fabric that is used on the long sides. This is cut 2¾in (8cm) wide. The binding is in darker red, this is also pieced.

If I'd had more of the brown fabric I would have made a slim brown border before the first white border. But I didn't, you use what you have!

Some of the blocks used in this quilt are shown with piecing diagrams, other blocks are described with instructions only.

Sawtooth star with a pinwheel centre
Cutting list:
- Cut the centre of the star, 5 x 5in (13.5 x 13.5cm)
- Cut four bottom pieces, 5 x 2¾in (13.5 x 7.75cm)
- Cut four squares, 2¾ x 2¾in (7.75 x 7.75cm)
- Cut eight star points, 2¾ x 2¾in (7.75 x 7.75cm)

Instructions:

See Old Blocks, New Quilt on pages 29–30. Replace the centre piece with a pinwheel made out of four half square triangle units. One half square triangle unit measures 2¼in (5.75cm) after it has been sewn into the quilt. I have drawn a sketch you can follow, see page 122. Put two fabrics right side to right side, trace the pattern and pin it on top. Sew on the dotted lines and cut along the lines. Tear off the paper, open the pieces and press. Trim the block to 2¾ x 2¾in (7.75 x 7.75cm).

Beacon light star

This block is sewn in four separate units – every star point has its own unit. The colour placement is shown on the diagram below. A full-size template is given on page 122.

Making the quilt

You will need:

Let's say you make 23 identical sawtooth stars (with solid not pinwheel centres), then the requirements would be as follows:
- Star centre pieces, 20in (50cm)
- Star points, 20in (50cm)
- Star bottom pieces, 32in (80cm)
- Brown filler fabric, 63in (160cm)
- Light border, 44in (110cm) (or 90in/230cm if you don't want to piece it)
- Red border, 32in (80cm) (or 90in/230cm if you don't want to piece it)
- Backing fabric, approximately 59 x 95in (150 x 240cm)
- Thick wadding (batting), queen size

When it came to the quilting I had it quilted on an industrial machine with a long arm.

The border was made by Anne-Kjersti, a very helpful and good worker. Thank you.

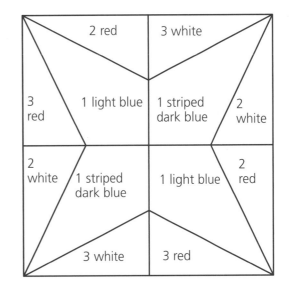

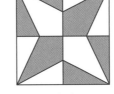

Beacon light star

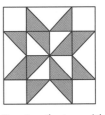

Sawtooth star with a pinwheel centre

2 red	3 white
3 red / 1 light blue	1 striped dark blue / 2 white
2 white / 1 striped dark blue	1 light blue / 2 red
3 white	3 red

Colour placement guide for beacon light star

Button Bag

Size: 12 x 11in (30 x 27cm) excluding handle.

You will need:
• Wool felt and cotton print fabric for the stripes, 12 pieces, 4in (10cm) of each
• Fabric for the lining, approximately 28 x 18in (70 x 45cm) (cut this after doing your own measurements)
• Fabric for the top edge, 6in (15cm)
• 30 buttons (five identical x 6)
• Ready-made leather bag handles, 8in (20cm)
• Cotton wadding (batting), 32 x 22in (80 x 55cm)
• Strong thread for the handle
• Magnetic snap closure

Cutting list:
• Cut 12 strips measuring 2½ x 11in (7 x 29.5cm), six in cotton prints and six in wool felt.
• Cut the top edge, 3¼in (9cm) wide.
• As an alternative to leather handles you can cut two linen handles, 27½ x 8in (70 x 20cm). Fold into eight layers and sew down the length of the handle. Hem along each short end

Instructions:
Sew the strips together vertically. Press the seam allowances against the cotton fabrics. Trim the edges straight if the strips have shifted slightly. Sew on the top edge piece. Attach the piece to the cotton wadding (batting) with tacking stitches. Quilt vertically down the cotton fabric a seam allowance distance from both long seams. Sew buttons onto the wool felt, leaving approximately 1¼in (5cm) at the bottom.

The lining has the same measurements as the sewn-together strips and is made separately. Visualize the exterior and lining as two table runners. Both are padded without backing. Sew all the decorations and any desired pockets/zips on the runners. Then sew each piece together along the short side so they become two separate cylinders. They now look pretty along the sides but are completely open at the top and bottom.

I have sewn a zip pocket in my bag lining, but this is optional. If you add one, it should be attached to the upper seam. Now it is all loose at the bottom and should be attached with two buttons sewn through the pocket and through the padded lining. Place the zip at least 2in (5cm) down from the upper edge.

Attach the bag closure. I used a magnetic snap that 'clicks' into the lining and through the wadding (batting). Place the other half on the reverse side and bend the metal prongs around. Position the prongs so they won't interfere with the top edge seam you will sew later. I suggest about 1½in (4cm) down. You can also find magnetic snaps that can be sewn on in the usual way at the very end of the process.

Sew together both cylinders at the top. (If you are using linen handles sew these into the seam. Ready-made leather handles should be sewn on by hand at the very end). Reverse one of the cylinders. Place them right sides together one inside the other. Push the handles in. Sew around the top. Turn the bag inside out so it looks like a bag, with the exception of the bottom which is still open.

Sew pretty stitching around the top of the bag. Choose stitch length 4 and a strong needle. Secure the threads somewhere that is not

very visible. If you are not sure if the stitching is going to look neat it's better to leave it. Alternatively you can stitch by hand with small, neat tacking stitches.

Put the bag on a table in front of you and cut away a small piece 1½ x 1in (3.75 x 2.5cm) from each bottom corner. Sew a zigzag seam along the edges at the bottom so the quilting

doesn't fray and the inside and outside cylinders stay in place. This makes it easier to sew the bottom together. Turn the bag inside out and sew the bottom together right side to right side. Sew a zigzag seam over the edge with a thread that matches the lining.

Turn the bag right side out and sew on the leather handles if you didn't use linen handles.

Easter Tablecloth

Size: approximately 35 x 35in (89 x 89cm) after washing and shrinkage.

Four old-fashioned fabrics and a border make this beautiful quintet. Begin by finding the fabrics for the nine-patch blocks. If you look closely at my fabrics, there is really nothing that tells you they will fit together. Flowery brown, yellow and pink together with a blue checked pattern aren't an obvious first choice! After sewing all the nine-patch blocks, measure them and cut filler squares the same size. Choose a filler that will make the nine-patch blocks look prettier. It can be a good idea to choose a colour that doesn't have any of the colours from the blocks in it. My filler fabric has yellow in it. As a border before the final row of blocks, I picked a lighter yellow with turquoise in the pattern. The outer border is bright blue to enclose the design. Refer to the pattern on page 127 before you continue reading.

Cut six 2in (6cm) strips of fabric, three light and three dark. Sew the strips together into two units (one light-dark-light and the other dark-light-dark) and cut the units into 2in (6cm) pieces. Sew these together as nine-patch blocks. Make 32 blocks. Measure the blocks and make 32 equal squares of the filler fabric. Sew together into a panel of six by six blocks. Cut a border measuring 3in (8.5cm). Sew this to the top and bottom of the panel. Sew another row of blocks onto the top and bottom. Attach a border to each long side. Sew together blocks for the long sides and include a piece of the border on each end. Sew onto the long sides.

The tablecloth is quilted in all seams. The yellow filler squares are quilted a seam allowance

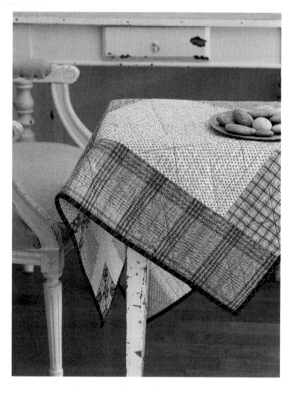

The front side of tablecloth is most likely the most important side, but I have to say that the back looks charming as well. Play with leftovers and don't stick to the rules, it's very liberating. Just put together large squares from your leftovers until the backing is big enough. Put some effort into piecing the backing in proportion to the front side. It only takes a few extra minutes.

distance from the seams and with a cross through the centre. The brown fabric in the nine-patch blocks is also quilted with a cross. The border is quilted with parallel lines. The yellow squares outside the border are quilted with parallel lines to match the border.

The pattern is on page 127.

Dedication

To my husband, our two great teenage girls and our little boy for showing respect for my train of thoughts. Interruptions in the process of writing a book can be very frustrating. I can have a whole instruction ready in my head, but as soon as anyone talks to me all the thoughts and words disappear and I have to start all over again. It takes time. With my workspace in the living room, I have come to appreciate a family that cares. Thanks to all four of you.

Suppliers

UK

Coast and Country Crafts
Barras Moor Farm
Perranarworthal
Truro TR3 7PE
T: 01872 870478
W: coastandcountrycrafts.co.uk

Creative Quilting
32 Bridge Road
East Molesey KT8 9HA
T: 020 941 7075
W: creativequilting.co.uk

Fred Aldous Ltd
37 Lever Street
Manchester M1 1LW
T: 0161 236 4224
W: fredaldous.co.uk

Panduro Hobby
Westway House
Transport Avenue
Brentford TW8 9HF
T: 020 8566 1680
W: panduro.co.uk

The Fat Quarters
5 Choprell Road
Blackhall Mill
Newcastle NE17 7TN
T: 01207 565728
W: thefatquarters.co.uk

The Sewing Bee
52 Hillfoot Street, Dunoon
Argyll PA23 7DS
T: 01369 706879
W: thesewingbee.co.uk

Threads and Patches
48 Aylesbury Street
Fenny Stratford
Bletchley MK2 2BU
T: 01908 649687
W: threadsandpatches.co.uk

EUROPE

Quiltzauberei.de
Marschallstr. 9
46539 Dinslaken, Germany
T: +49 2064 827980
W: quiltzauberei.de

USA

Coats and Clark
PO Box 12229
Greenville SC 29612-0229
T: 0800 648 1479
W: coatsandclark.com

Connecting Threads
13118 NE 4th Street
Vancouver
WA 98684
T: 1-800-574-6454
W: connectingthreads.com

eQuilter.com
5455 Spine Road, Suite E
Boulder CO 80301
T: 303-527-0856
W: eQuilter.com

J&O Fabrics
9401 Rt.130
Pennsauken
NJ 08110
T: 856-633-2121
W: jandofabrics.com

Patterns

All patterns are shown at full size, excluding the 'Denim Patch' pattern on page 118.

Pocket Pooch

Hand-Sewn Coaster

Cute Sweater

Simple Pincushions

Boy's Pyjamas

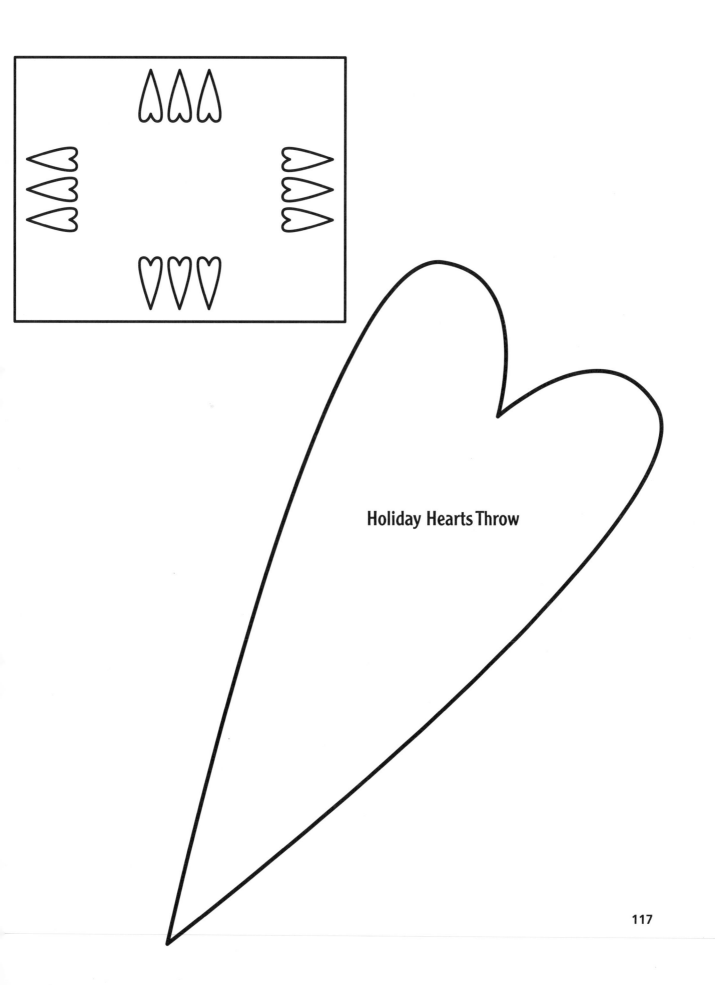

Holiday Hearts Throw

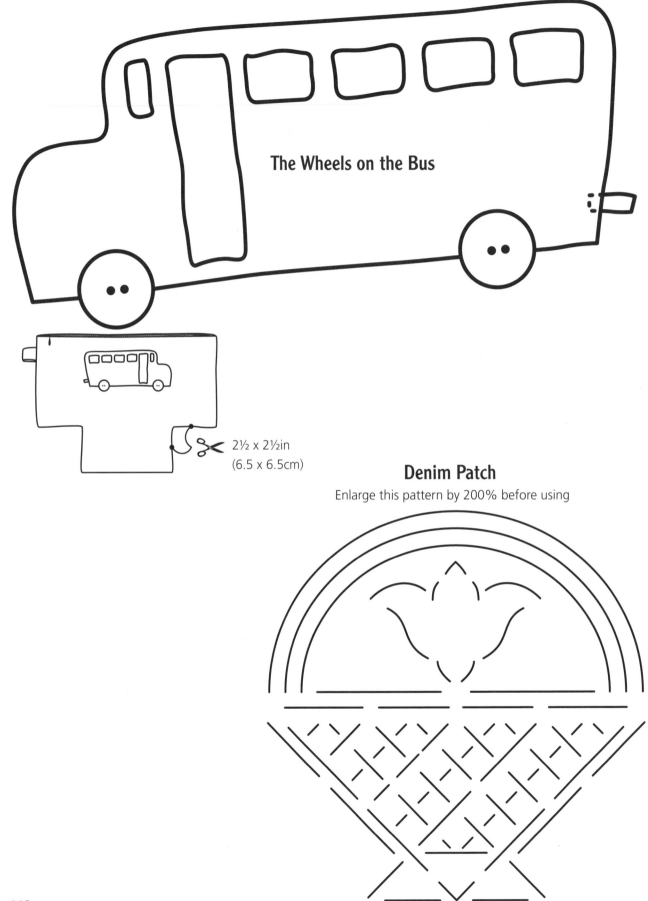

The Wheels on the Bus

2½ x 2½in
(6.5 x 6.5cm)

Denim Patch

Enlarge this pattern by 200% before using

Home is Best' Cushion

Internet Stars Quilt
– pinwheel centre

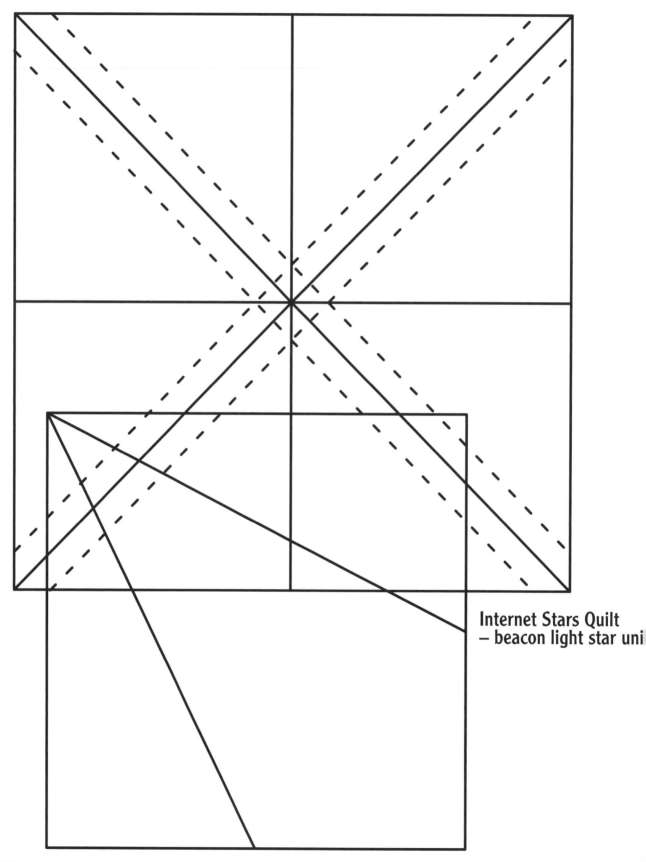

Internet Stars Quilt
– beacon light star uni

Hearts on Squares

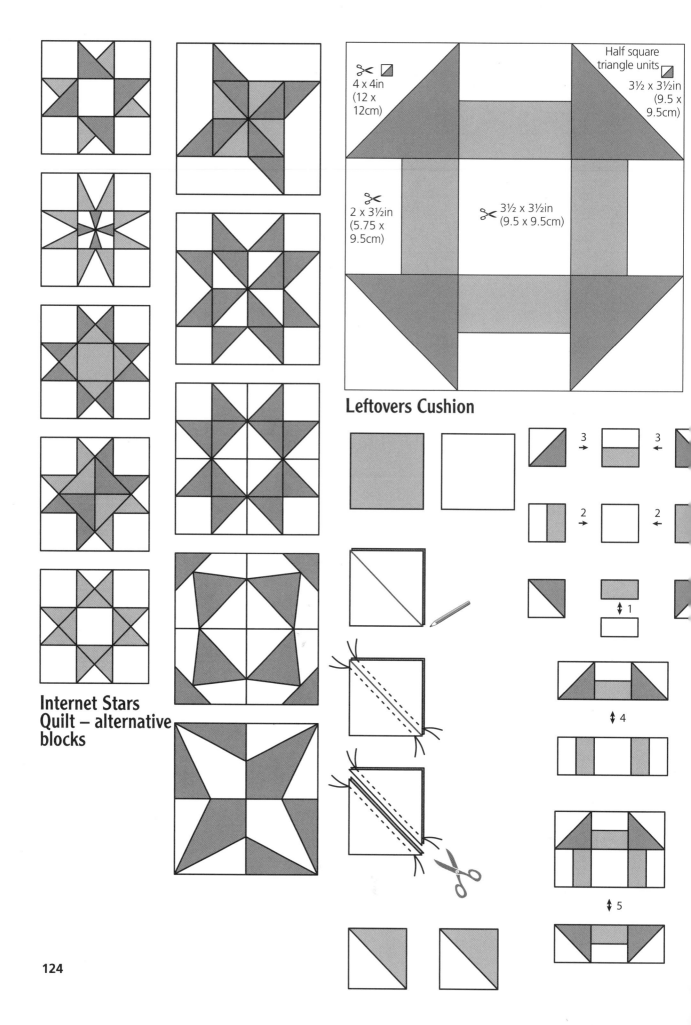

Leftovers Cushion

Half square triangle units

✂ 4 x 4in (12 x 12cm)

3½ x 3½in (9.5 x 9.5cm)

✂ 2 x 3½in (5.75 x 9.5cm)

✂ 3½ x 3½in (9.5 x 9.5cm)

Internet Stars Quilt – alternative blocks

Appliqué Tea Towels

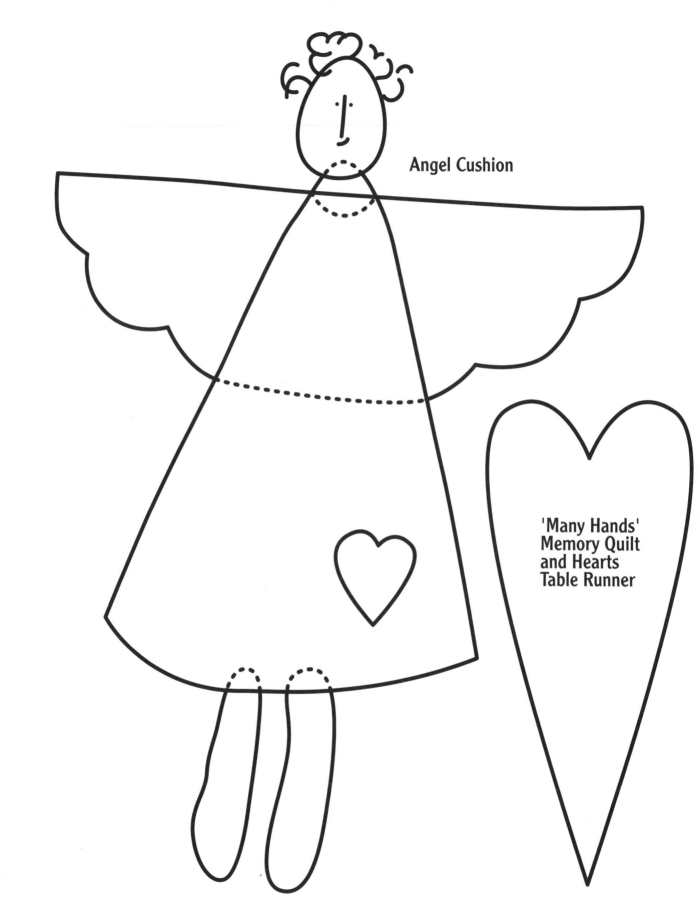

Angel Cushion

'Many Hands'
Memory Quilt
and Hearts
Table Runner

126

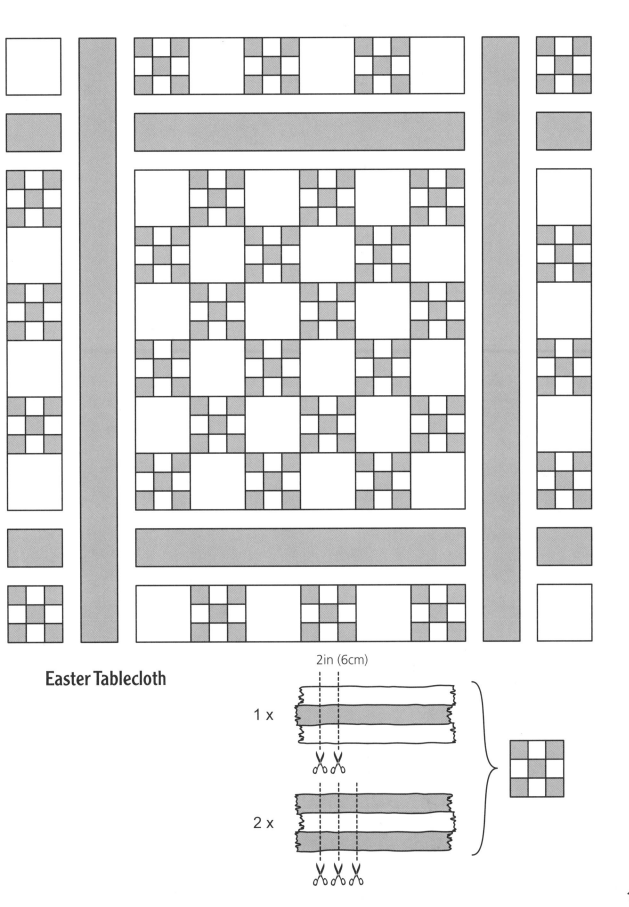

Easter Tablecloth

2in (6cm)

1 x

2 x

Index

adhesive 22, 25, 28, 86
angels 90–1, 92–3, 95, 125–6
appliqué, machine/hand 27

backing fabric 14, 32
bags
  button 110–11
  mini purses 52–9
  shoulder 50–1
  tea-towel tote 34–5
blocks
  choosing/arranging 10, 11
  leftover 29, 66, 85, 103
boat, embroidered 74, 116
books 22–3, 25
borders 11, 18–19, 20, 70–3
bracelet, button 77
bus appliqué 68–9, 118
buttons
  bag 110–11
  bracelet 77
  keyring 74
  matchboxes 22
  mittens 76
  wall art 24–5, 44–5, 87

Christmas 22–5, 27, 36–7
churn dash blocks 10, 85
coaster, hand-sewn 74, 116
colour 12–13, 73
cot blanket 70–2
cushions
  alphabet 66–7
  angel 2, 90–1, 125–6
  Christmas 36–7
  Home is Best 60–3, 119–21
  leftovers 84–5, 124
  summer 38

denim patch 88, 118
dog, appliqué emblem 39, 116
doll's quilt 64–5

Easter 102, 112–13, 123, 127
embroidery 29, 43–4, 74
equipment 8, 9, 14, 17, 25

fabric
  choosing 8, 12–13, 14, 73
  fillers 10, 11
  recycling 38, 42, 66, 73, 85
false bottoms 34, 56, 78
four-patch blocks 10, 29–31,
    78, 102, 103

handmade quilts 14, 27, 40
hearts
  embroidery picture 29
  memory quilt 96–9
  pincushions 75, 116
  potholder 95
  squares quilt 26–8, 123
  table runner 100–1
  tea towel 92–3, 125
  throw 40–1, 117

jars, needlework 80–2
joint projects 40, 75, 96, 108

key ring 74

letters 60–3, 66–7, 119–21
log cabin 10, 80–3, 105–7

machine-made quilts 14–19
matchboxes 22, 25
measurements 9
mittens, buttons 76

nine-patch block 10, 112

paper aids 18–19, 27, 105
patterns
  fabric 12–13, 17
  stitching 17–18
  transfering 9, 18
pencil case 52–6, 68–9
picture frames 22, 29, 82, 87
pig, picture frame 82–3
pincushions 75, 78–82, 116
planning projects 8, 10
potholders 94–5
pram quilt 103–4

purses, mini 52–9, 68–9, 77
puss in the corner block 10, 46
pyjamas, truck 89–90, 116

quilt code 14–19
quilts
  beautiful borders 70–3
  boy's stuff 46–9
  cot blanket 70–2
  doll's 64–5
  hearts on squares 26–8, 123
  memory, hearts 96–9, 127
  pram 103–4
  star blocks 29–33, 108–9,
      122, 124

recycling 38, 42, 66, 73,
    85, 100
ribbon 22, 74, 78, 92

sawtooth star block 10, 108–9
seam allowance 9
sewing machine 8, 14, 18, 19,
    27, 32
stabilizers 9, 27, 86
star blocks quilts 29–33, 108–9,
    122, 124
stitching 14, 17, 19
suppliers 114
sweater, appliqué 86, 116

table runner 100–1, 105, 107
table topper 102, 106–7, 123
tablecloth 70–2, 112–13, 127
tacking 19
tags 32
tea towels 34–5, 92–3, 125
thread 14, 19, 32
throw, hearts 40–1, 117
truck 89–90, 116

wall decorations 24, 25,
    42–5, 87
washing 19

zip fasteners 54–6